D1596470

# ABOUT THIS BOOK

Paris: the City of Light and Love. The French capital has been praised in song, served as a backdrop for films and plays, and inspired novels and plays more than perhaps any other city in the world. The historic center of Paris includes the banks of the Seine between Pont de Sully and Pont d'Iéna as well as its magnificent monuments, all of which are featured in the UNESCO World Heritage List. Notre-Dame on the Île de la Cité, the Louvre and the Jardin des Tuil-

eries, the magnificent bridges and of course the Eiffel Tower invite visitors to take memorable strolls and experience the history and tradition. The masterpieces in the Louvre set not only experts in raptures; the Centre Pompidou is also a cultural magnet at the heart of a lively scene. In the Musée Orsay you can admire a world-famous collection of Impressionist paintings; in the Musée Rodin you will be fascinated by the impressive sculptures of Auguste

Rodin. Elegant squares and broad avenues as well as romantic districts like Le Marais and the Quartier Latin, the historic university district, form the extremes in this expanding political, economic and cultural arena. And yet, the individual districts can still be conveniently explored on foot. When your feet ache from all the walking, you can take refuge in the Métro, for it is said that no point in Paris lies further than 500 meters from one of its stations. Paris claims to be the most French of all the cities in France. At the same time it is the most international of all French cities – not only because of the many visitors who come here each year, but because Paris, as a center of culture, intellect and lifestyle has always attracted countless artists, scholars and anyone hungry for a taste of life from another part of the world.

From the original settlement on the Île de la Cité, the city on the Seine grew to become a vast urban entity. "Province remains province; it makes itself ridiculous when it attempts to imitate Paris," observed Honoré de Balzac. Even back in his day, it was here, in the heart of France, that you could feel the pulse of the "Grande Nation".

# TABLE OF CONTENTS

"Nobody should presume to have a firm opinion about life, love or literature before visiting Paris..." (Djuna Barnes)

Photos on the previous pages:

p. 1 The face of the Louvre: Mona Lisa
p. 2/3 The icon of the city: the Eiffel Tower
p. 4/5 Rue Edouard Quenu in the Quartier Latin
p. 6/7 Rue Norvins on Montmartre with a view of the Sacré-Cœur
p. 8/9 La Défense: soaring modern buildings and Mitterrand's "Cube" (Grande Arche)

# ÎLE DE LA CITÉ, ÎLE SAINT-LOUIS, RIVE DROITE

Two islands on the River Seine – the Île de la Cité and Île Saint-Louis – form the heart of Paris. The Celtic Parisii people settled here around 300 BC, and remained there until the Romans came and took over the area. Construction of a royal palace and the Cathédrale Notre-Dame de Paris in the Middle Ages made the Île de la Cité the undisputed focal point of political and religious power. Today, the Right Bank (Rive Droite) is home to the Élysée Palace, official residence of the French president, and the Champs-Élysées, with its elegant boutiques and upscale clientele.

This evening view takes in the Centre Pompidou, the illuminated city center and the eastern end of the Île de la Cité, which is connected to the smaller Île Saint-Louis by the Pont Saint-Louis.

# ÎLE SAINT-LOUIS, ÎLE DE LA CITÉ

Originally, there were three islands in the River Seine, which flows through the heart of Paris. The two smaller islands – the Île aux Vaches and the Île Notre-Dame – were connected in 1614, and in 1725 the joint island was renamed Île Saint-Louis. While the Île de la Cité attracts visitors to its important historic monuments, people come to the Île Saint-Louis to stroll through its tranquil streets lined with palaces from the 17th and 18th centuries. In the mid-19th century, poet Charles Baudelaire wrote his weighty volume Les fleurs du mal (Flowers of Evil) in the Hôtel de Lauzun here. In more recent times, the Île Saint-Louis has still had its share of noteworthy residents, including Georges Pompidou, the French president after whom the cultural complex was named, film actor Jean-Claude Brialy, and singer Georges Moustaki.

From one end of the Île Saint-Louis you get a wonderful view over the Île de la Cité and the Cathédrale Notre-Dame de Paris (below). Pont Neuf, the oldest bridge in Paris (left), spans the river at the western tip of the Île de la Cité. Small shops and bistros create a cozy atmosphere in the narrow roads of the Île Saint-Louis, which were first built at the beginning of the 17th century.

# THE RIVER, THE GODDESS AND ITS (BEACH) LOVERS

The Seine rises northwest of Dijon, in Burgundy, and flows into the English Channel near Le Havre, in a delta crossed by three bridges. Its total length of 776 km (485 mi) makes it the second-longest river in France after the Loire. As such, the Seine has played an important role since the early days of European civilization. The Gallo-Romans even worshiped "Dea Sequana" (goddess of the Seine), and for Paris, which owns the springs of the Seine to

this day, it was an important transport route – the city's coat of arms still features a ship and its motto is "Fluctuat, nec mergitur" (shaken by the waves, but it will not sink). That must be what Paul Celan was thinking when he wrote these lines: "Paris, the ship, lies at anchor on the glassy water / I sit at table with you and drink to you / I drink until my heart darkens for you / until Paris swims on its tears / until it sets sail for the distant veil / in which

the world envelops us, where every You is a branch / on which I hang as a leaf that hovers in silence". In 1991, UNESCO added the banks of the Seine in Paris to the World Cultural Heritage list. During the summer months, sand is spread here so that the Parisians can enjoy a taste of "beach life" in the heart of the city. There are even plans to transform the roads along the river banks, despite their heavy traffic, into a permanent pedestrian zone.

# THE RIVER, THE GODDESS AND ITS (BEACH) LOVERS

The Île de la Cité and the Notre-Dame de Paris sit in the river like a ship at anchor. The view from the Quai d'Orléans toward the Île Saint-Louis (left) offers a grand view of the apse on the east side of the church. Below: The Quai des Orfèvres (goldsmiths' quay), was the center for jewelers in Paris during the 17th and 18th centuries, and leads to Pont St-Michel, built in 1857 to replace an older bridge built in 1378.

# NOTRE-DAME DE PARIS

Notre-Dame de Paris – more accurately the square in front of it – is not only the focal point of Paris, it is the geographical hub of the whole country. A metal plate set in the ground there marks the spot from which every point in France is measured. Completed in 1345 (the foundation stone was laid by Bishop Maurice de Sully in 1163), the western façade of this Gothic masterpiece has a wealth of sculptures. Above the three carved portals, which represent the life of the Virgin, the life of St Anne, and the Last Judgement, are figures in the Gallery of Kings. These are reproductions, however, as the originals were decapitated in the Revolution – a few of the heads are on display in the Musée de Cluny. The interior, partially redesigned in the 18th century, has an impressive, solemn atmosphere that is emphasized when the great organ sounds for services or concerts.

# NOTRE-DAME DE PARIS

The Gothic Cathédrale Notre-Dame de Paris dominates the dramatic view from the banks of the Seine (left). The distinctive towers, which Victor Hugo once called a "harmonious part of a magnificent whole", measure a total of 69 m (226 ft) high. In the middle of the choir room, raised on semi-circular marble steps, stands the main altar, featuring a pietà by Nicolas Coustou (1658–1733) (below).

# VICTOR HUGO AND *THE HUNCHBACK OF NOTRE-DAME*

In his novel *Notre-Dame de Paris* (1831), Victor Hugo (1802–1885) managed to craft an important monument to the medieval city. It was only later, for the translation, that the book was renamed *The Hunchback of Notre Dame*. It has been filmed on several occasions since then, as well as adapted for the stage, but interestingly, the sad saga of the hunchbacked Quasimodo is not the main focus of the original novel. The central emphasis is really a eulogy of Gothic architecture, of which Hugo was an enthusiastic fan. "He who is born a poet will become an architect," he once proclaimed. Born the son of a general, he travelled extensively in his youth and grew up partly in Italy and Spain. He was politically active his whole life and was not afraid to confront injustices. In 1851, he fled the country after the Louis Napoléon Bonaparte coup, who then crowned himself Emperor Napoleon III. His first stop was Brussels, followed by Jersey in the Channel Islands. He then lived on the island of Guernsey, from 1855 until his return to Paris in 1871. In his later years, he became actively involved in politics once again, and in 1876 was elected into the Senate. Victor Hugo also wrote numerous poems and successful plays. His work *Le roi s'amuse* (1832) provided the model for Verdi's opera *Rigoletto*.

# VICTOR HUGO AND *THE HUNCHBACK OF NOTRE-DAME*

France's admiration for Victor Hugo is still strong, as can be seen at his home on Place des Vosges, which is now a museum (below). The house provides insight into the writer's lifestyle, while his literary salon was at Rue de Clichy 21, where the intellectual élite of the city met back in the day. (Left: an illustration by the artist Eugène Devéria in one edition of *The Hunchback of Notre-Dame.*

# SAINTE-CHAPELLE

King Louis IX (1226–1270) had the "Holy Chapel" built on the grounds of his residence in just thirty-three months, between 1245 and 1248, as a place of safekeeping for valuable Byzantine relics he had "collected". These were then kept in the upper part of the chapel, to which only the king had access, while the lower part was used by the people at court. The church is 33 m (108 ft) long and 17 m (56 ft) high, and is surmounted by a 76-m-high (250-ft) spire. The stained glass windows are the oldest in Paris, and of the 1,134 scenes covering an area of 618 sq m (6,652 sq ft), an impressive 720 originals have survived; the rest were destroyed during fires in the 17th and 18th centuries. The sunlight that filters through them shines on fourteen Gothic pillars, each 22 m (72 ft) tall, which rise in the upper chapel to form a blue, cross-ribbed vault dotted with golden stars.

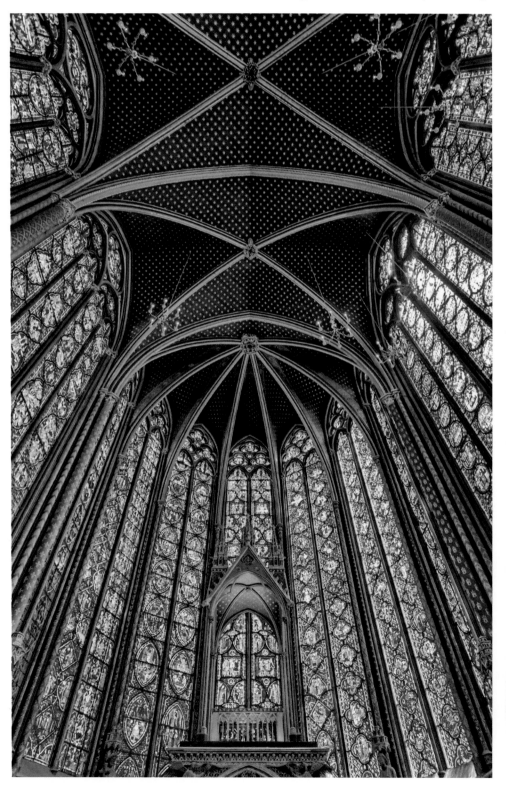

The High-Gothic Sainte-Chapelle is one of the most beautiful places of worship in France. When the sunlight shines through the elaborate tracery of the stained glass windows, it creates iridescent patterns of light (below). The impression of space in the two parts of the church varies considerably. the lower church (left) is considerably lower and darker than the upper church because of its smaller windows.

# CONCIERGERIE

Just like Sainte-Chapelle, the Conciergerie is also part of the palace belonging to the Capetian (Merovingian) dynasty. The complex consisting of three buildings was constructed by Philipp IV (1285–1314, known as Philip the Fair) in the High Gothic style around 1300. At the end of the 14th century, the first public clock was mounted on one of the round towers, the Tour de l'Horloge. La Conciergerie was the official seat of the "Concierge", the steward of the royal palace, who exercised the rule of law on behalf of the monarch. The building was thus also a prison in the Middle Ages. During the Revolution it was infamous as the "antechamber to the guillotine": Marie-Antoinette, Danton and Robespierre were all jailed in the Salle des Girondins (former chapel), condemned to death in the Salle des Gens d'Armes (former dining room) and led along the Rue de Paris to the scaffold.

On the western tip of the Île de la Cité, directly behind the massive arches of the Pont Neuf, is the riverside Quai de l'Horloge. It acquired its name from the imposing corner tower of the Conciergerie with the city's first public clock (left). It is here that you now find the entrance to the building, which is a museum that is also a venue for classical concert performances.

# HÔTEL DE VILLE

The Hôtel de Ville, the town hall of Paris, is a late-19th-century building that was designed in its present form, the neo-Renaissance style, by architects Théodore Ballu and Edouard Deperthes. The previous building, a Renaissance palais, was destroyed during the uprising of the Paris Commune in 1871. The façade of the current town hall is adorned with 146 statues representing important Parisian personalities, including painter Eu-

gène Delacroix, historian and writer Jules Michelet, actor François-Joseph Talma, sculptor Jean-Baptiste Pigalle, Versailles garden architect André Le Nôtre, and Cardinal Richelieu. Since 1977, it has served as the residence of the mayor of Paris – before that the city was headed by a prefect, like all the other départements in France; only the individual arrondissements of Paris actually had their own mayors.

For centuries, executions were held on the square in front of the richly decorated town hall – François Ravaillac, who assassinated King Henri IV, was tied and quartered here in 1610. The stately hall inside (below) is also a popular venue for cultural events.

# LE MARAIS

The street now known as Rue Saint-Antoine is one of the oldest in Paris. It was built in Roman times just slightly raised above the marshy district (Le Marais) to protect it from flooding. In the 13th century, monks and Templar Knights settled here and drained the surrounding land, making it arable as well as suitable for construction. The aristocracy later built magnificent mansions here, but they were driven out during the French Revolution, when large numbers of craftsmen settled in Le Marais, east of Beaubourg between the Place de la République and the Place de la Bastille. The fact that it is one of the most desirable districts in the capital, with designer boutiques, galleries, markets and restaurants, is due in part to writer André Malraux, who had the area renovated during the early 1960s when he was Minister of Culture.

There is no sign of the old rose bushes that gave this street its name, Rue des Rosiers. Nonetheless, with its little cobblestone alleys and squares, tiny bookshops and kosher restaurants, Le Marais still looks as if time has stood still for the past 100 years. Many artists and urbanites have also settled in the district.

# THE SECRET CAPITAL OF EUROPEAN JEWS

Of the roughly 800,000 members of the Jewish community in France today, almost half lives in Paris. They have been drawn to the city on the Seine since the 13th century: initially Sephardim (descendants of Jews from Spain and Portugal until their expulsion in 1492 and 1531), and later Ashkenazim (Jews from Eastern Central and Central Europe). The heart of Jewish Paris beats in the "Pletzl" – the Yiddish name for the district around the Rue des Rosiers. Le Marais is also home to the Agudath-Hakehiloth Synagogue (also called the Synagogue de la Rue Pavée), designed in 1913 by Art-Nouveau architect Hector Guimard, who married a Jewish artist. It was burned down during the German occupation and then rebuilt as a monument after World War II. In the vicinity you will find kosher restaurants and food shops, Jewish publishing companies and bookshops as well as the Hôtel Saint-Aignan, erected during the 17th century. The latter now houses a museum of Jewish art and history that also shows works by Modigliani and Chagall. However, the biggest synagogue in Paris is not in Le Marais, but on the Rue la Victoire in the 8th arrondissement. Consecrated in 1874, the high vaulted roof of the neo-Romanesque "Grande Synagogue de Paris" provides space for a congregation of 2,000.

# THE SECRET CAPITAL OF EUROPEAN JEWS

The inside of the "Synagoge de la Rue Notre-Dame-de-Nazareth" shines brightly during services (below). Dedicated in 1852, it is the oldest surviving synagogue in Paris. The Bar-Mitzvah (from Hebrew meaning "Son of the Commandment") is a rite of passage for boys that is usually held on the Sabbath after his thirteenth birthday (left).

# ARISTOCRATIC CITY PALACES IN LE MARAIS

Le Marais has been part of Paris since the construction of the "new" city wall in the 14th century. The district was given this status when Charles V (1364–1380, known as the Wise) left the royal palace on the Île de la Cité and moved into the Hôtel St-Paul, between the Rue St-Antoine and the road along the banks of the Seine. His son Charles VI, who ascended the throne in 1380, at the age of only twelve, is said to have made the palace into a "mad-house". In the following period, Le Marais became the focal point of courtly life. Magnificent city palaces were built, including the Hôtel de Sens, the Hôtel de Sully, the Hôtel de Soubise and the Hôtel Carnavalet, which was built from 1548 for Jacques de Ligneris, president of the parliament of Paris at the time. In 1578, Carnavalet came under the ownership of Françoise de la Baume-Montrevel, widow of the Sire de Kernevenoy, whose Breton name was modified to become the French "Carnavalet". There is, however, a more amusing legend regarding the name, which told that the 19-year-old widow was so bored in her palace that the courtiers decided to cheer her up by introducing crowds of admirers, whose costumes became increasingly extravagant in the attempt to outdo each other that their arrival resembled a carnival procession.

# ARISTOCRATIC CITY PALACES IN LE MARAIS

Many of the aristocratic palaces in Le Marais were built during the 17th and 18th centuries and are open to the public today. The statue of Louis XIV in the middle of the courtyard (below), created by the sculptor Antoine Coysevox, was previously in the Hôtel de Ville.

# PLACE DE LA BASTILLE

The Bastille was built in the 14th century under Charles V as part of the city's fortifications. His successors then extended it to create a mighty prison with eight fortified towers. In 1789, the spark that fired the Revolution came from the storming of the Bastille complex, where famous personalities such as Voltaire, Mirabeau and the Marquis de Sade had been imprisoned. Although the building was demolished, the square retained its symbolic character and is still a very important gathering place for Parisians every year on July 14, a national holiday. In the middle of the Place de la Bastille stands the *Colonne de Juillet* (July Column), a 47-m (150-ft) monument completed in 1840 that recalls the July Revolution of 1830. Directly on the spot of the former prison, on the southeast side of the square, is the new opera house, the Opéra Bastille.

The Bastille, after which the square is named, was razed in 1789/1790. The gilded statue on the July Column recalls the Spirit of Freedom (Le Génie de la Liberté). It was created by Augustin-Alexandre Dumont, the scion of a family of famous French artists who established his own studio in Paris after studying in Rome for seven years.

# "BORN FREE": THE FRENCH REVOLUTION

For years, the "ordinary people" had been growing increasingly discontented. They had bourne the entire tax burden of the state to finance the extravagant lifestyles of the monarchy while the aristocracy and the clergy were exempt from payment. A massive increase in the price of bread further fuelled their disaffection and, although there is no proof that the much-quoted comment by Queen Marie-Antoinette was actually uttered ("...if the people had no bread they should eat cake instead"), the prevailing attitude among the wealthy ultimately led to the storming of the Bastille on July 14, 1789. Despite fewer than ten prisoners being held at the time, this is unanimously regarded as the beginning of the French Revolution. Demolition of the hated prison building began just two days later, but the most important (intellectual) event occurred on August 26, 1789, when the National Assembly passed the declaration of human and civic rights (included in the first French constitution of 1791). It is one of the fundamentally democratic texts ever written, and was used in 1948 as the basis for the Universal Declaration of Human Rights of the United Nations. Article One of this declaration states: "All human beings are born free and equal in dignity and rights".

# "BORN FREE": THE FRENCH REVOLUTION

The events of the French Revolution – from the storming of the Bastille (opposite page, top and bottom) to the execution of Louis XVI (left) inspired many artists. One of the most famous works produced during this time is the painting by Eugène Delacroix from 1830: Liberty Leading the People (below).

# OPÉRA BASTILLE

By the early 1980s, the old opera house, the Opéra Garnier, had become far too small to provide the capital with a satisfactory program. The French president at the time, François Mitterand, therefore commissioned a new opera house in 1983. It was built over a period of six years on the site of the former Bastille station on the Place de la Bastille. Today, together with the old Opéra Garnier, it forms the Opéra national de Paris. While the Opéra Garnier mostly shows ballet productions nowadays, the Opéra Bastille, which was opened in 1989, provides enough space for more elaborate opera productions within a steel, concrete and glass building that is filled with light and covers an area of 22,000 sq m (236,800 sq ft). There is a large auditorium with 2,700 seats, an amphitheater with 450 seats and the studio with 237 seats.

World-famous opera stars appear on stage at the Opéra Bastille, including Chinese-Canadian soprano Zhang Liping, who gave a brilliant performance in Paris in Giacomo Puccini's *Madame Butterfly* (below). The modern building was designed by Canadian-Uruguayan architect Carlos Ott with glass façades and looks particularly attractive when it is illuminated for the evening performances (left).

# AMÉLIE AND THE OTHERS: PARIS ON THE BIG SCREEN

French film has a long tradition. It began in 1885 with the Lumière brothers, who made short features such as *L'Arroseur arrosé*. The French film industry developed quickly thereafter, holding its own in the global market; even during World War II, masterpieces such as *Les Enfants du Paradis* took audiences by storm. A high point then came at the end of the 1950s and start of the 1960s, when films by the Nouvelle Vague (French New Wave) attract-ed worldwide attention. Technical innovations enabled film crews to move out of the studios and onto the streets, thus capturing the atmosphere of the city. Locations (typically Paris) frequently became the star of the film, or at least a major feature within it. The Antoine Doinel films by François Truffaut – the most famous of which is *Les Quatre Cent Coups* (The 400 Blows) – are a good example of the Nouvelle Vague. More recent films focusing on the French capital include *Les Amants du Pont Neuf* (The Lovers on the Bridge) by Léos Carax, *Le Fabuleux Destin d'Amélie Poulain* (Amélie) by Jean-Pierre Jeunet, and the 2008 romantic comedy *Paris* by Cédric Klapisch. Visitors can even catch the latest releases of British and American films in English – look out for "vo" (version originale) in the description, which indicates the film has subtitles in French and is not dubbed.

# AMÉLIE AND THE OTHERS: PARIS ON THE BIG SCREEN

Films shape our image of a city. "Amélie", for example, was partially shot in the Café des deux Moulins near the Gare du Nord station (amongst other places), where today a film poster signed by actress Audrey Tautou hangs on the wall (below). But films are also inspired by the image of a city, such as Vincente Minnelli's *An American in Paris* (1951) starring Gene Kelly (left).

# PLACE DES VOSGES

The oldest square in Paris goes back to King Henri IV (1553–1610), who had a vast complex built in a still delightfully secluded area, and which is accessible only through gateways to the north and south. Plans for the ensemble began in 1605, and after its completion in 1612 it quickly became a popular meeting point for Paris' elite. The uniform design of the thirty-six pavilion façades around the square "Place Royale", as the square was originally called, are thought to have been designed by Androuet du Cerceau or Louis Métezeau. Either way, they can be traced back to a corresponding wish of the king. It was only in 1800 that it acquired its present name, in honour of the département Vosges, which had been the first to pay its taxes. Among the famous residents of the square were writers Victor Hugo, Théophile Gautier and Alphonse Daudet.

At the center of the Place des Vosges is a green space with a pretty fountain surrounded by a railing. Beneath the massive arcades are a number of restaurant options for visitors to explore. The most exclusive (and expensive) venue is the three-star restaurant L'Ambroisie (9 Place des Vosges), where classics such as lobster fricassée with chestnuts and squash, or Bresse poultry with crayfish are on the menu.

# THE (STARRY) SKIES ABOVE PARIS

"To live like a bee in clover" – applied to France, most people would think of French cuisine and the numerous important restaurants in the country, many of which are in Paris. Two institutions are responsible for evaluating restaurants in France: Michelin, which awards them with stars, and Gault-Millau, which awards restaurants with chef's toques. Their judgments are based on the freshness of the products as well as on the skills of the preparation and creativity of the chefs. A long tradition of quality does not count: the Tour d'Argent, for many years the most famous restaurant in Paris, has lost two of its three stars over the past fifteen years. In 2010, the Michelin guide awarded three stars to ten restaurants in Paris, thirteen were awarded two stars and forty-one gained one star; these gourmet temples are scattered across all the arrondissements of the city.

A special combination of pleasure and ambience can be experienced at "Le Jules Verne" by starred chef Alain Ducasse – it is located 125 m (412 ft) up the Eiffel Tower. Chefs in this superior category an also charge superior prices in their establishments, but for those who cannot, or would rather not, spend quite so much money, should make enquiries – some starred restaurants also run a second, less expensive option.

Gourmets hoping to test the culinary skills of Frédéric Anton in Le Pré Catelan (left), can combine it with an excursion to Paris's green outskirts – the restaurant lies in the Bois de Boulogne. Beneath the arcades of the Place des Vosges is the realm of Bernard Pacaud, L'Ambroisie (below left). The sommeliers are always ready to give you expert advice on the right wines as well (below).

# MUSÉE PICASSO

The Musée Picasso owes its foundation to a law that was passed in France in 1971, decreeing that heirs can also pay inheritance tax by transferring the ownership of their artworks to the state. Since artist Pablo Picasso (living in France at the time) kept a large number of his masterpieces for himself, however, some cynical souls maintain that the law was passed specifically with a view to gaining possession of his estate. When Picasso died in 1973, the French state thus acquired an extensive collection of works by the master (paintings, sculptures and pottery). They were initially exhibited in the Grand Palais before finding their final home in 1985 at the Hôtel Salé in Le Marais, which was specially rebuilt to house them. In the summer of 2009, the museum was closed due to major renovations, but they are expected to be completed by the spring of 2013.

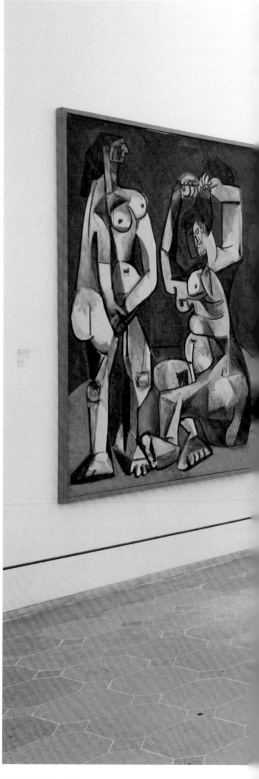

The Hôtel Salé was built by tax collector Pierre Aubert around 1660. The name is a reference to the fact that Aubert's prime job was the collection of salt taxes. The magnificent building, with its grand staircase, had a succession of owners until it was acquired in 1962 by the city of Paris. Following restoration work, Picasso's masterpieces – both sculptures and paintings – found a permanent home there.

# MUSÉE DES ARTS ET MÉTIERS

Anyone who has read Umberto Eco's novel *Foucault's Pendulum* will be familiar with the Musée des Arts et Métiers. Founded in 1794, it is here that the most exciting scenes in the novel take place, and it is here that you can see the pendulum with which physicist Léon Foucault proved the rotation of the earth in 1851 in Paris. The basis of the museum is the collection of the Conservatoire National des Arts et Métiers, established by Abbé Henri Grégoire; it is one of the most important arts and crafts colleges in Paris. The exhibits are displayed in the medieval rooms of the Abbey of Saint-Martin-des-Champs, which was secularized during the French Revolution. It contains significant reminders of major scientific inventions such as Daguerre's dark room, the cinematograph of the Lumière brothers, Watt's steam engine and many other interesting objects.

Apart from the exhibits themselves, the halls of the Musée des Arts et Métiers are worth a visit in their own right. The spacious and stylish presentation of the collection, which features a well-organized overview of the development of science and inventions up until and including the Industrial Revolution. Here you can also see the first model of the Statue of Liberty, made by Frédéric-Auguste Bartholdi in 1870.

# CENTRE POMPIDOU

Opened in 1977, the Centre Pompidou was initially greeted by a resoundingly negative response. The building by Renzo Piano and Richard Rogers, whose brightly colored service lines run along the exterior, reminded rather cynical critics of an oil refinery or a "fridge from behind". Since then, however, the cultural center named after a former French president has long become one of the most popular sights in the city. It is home to the Musée National d'Art Moderne, with a number of special exhibitions, a center for industrial design, a library, an arthouse cinema, and the IRCAM (Institut de Recherche et Coordination Acoustique / Musique) as well as an art bookshop, an internet café, a café and a restaurant. The escalators, which also run on the outside of the building through perspex tubes, afford magnificent views across the rooftops of Paris.

From the inside, the angular steel girder construction of the Centre Pompidou, with its large areas of glass and high ceilings, rather resembles a convention center. The impression of transparency is accented by the perspex tubes containing the escalators. The Stravinsky Fountain on the square in front of the building was created by the artist team of Niki de Saint-Phalle and Jean Tinguely in 1982 and 1983.

# FORUM DES HALLES

This was once the site of a covered market (Les Halles), consisting originally of twelve buildings constructed of metal and glass between 1852 and 1936 based on designs by Victor Baltard. They were a hive of activity then, but by the 1960s they had become too small for the needs of the growing city. The wholesale market was thus moved – not without noisy protests – to Rungis in the south of Paris, and the old Les Halles were given over to the wrecking ball. They were ultimately replaced by the Forum des Halles, a shopping center with over 160 shops, banks, a post office, several cinemas, restaurants, the largest Olympic-size swimming pool in Paris (50 meters in length), a big fitness center and numerous event venues. The roofs of the Forum have been turned into a park criss-crossed by footpaths.

One of the main attractions for younger visitors to the Forum des Halles is the old-fashioned carousel. Typical of the four-storey, partly subterranean shopping center are the glass roofs, which are supported by white arches. On the edge of the Forum is Saint-Eustache, a Gothic church in which Louis XIV, Madame de Pompadour and Molière were all baptized.

# SAINT-EUSTACHE

Saint-Eustache stands firm beside the gleaming chrome construction of the Forum des Halles – a sturdy bastion of faith. The church was built along the lines of Notre-Dame de Paris between 1532 and 1640, on the ruins of a little chapel dedicated to Saint Agnes. The new place of worship was dedicated to Saint Eustachius, a former Roman general who converted to Christianity towards the end of the first century and who was later martyred. The church was paid for by the merchants and guilds from Les Halles, and by King François I (1515–1547). Its Gothic origins can be seen above all in the soaring, 34-m-high (112-ft) nave of the cruciform church, which covers an area of 3,872 sq m (41,677 sq ft). In 1855, Hector Berlioz' *Te Deum* was performed for the first time on the famous Ducroquet-Gonzalès organ, as was Liszt's *Missa Solemnis* (Messe de Gran) in 1866.

The Parish Church of Saint-Eustache is an
architectural masterpiece, and not only when it
is illuminated at night. Because it was built over
a long period of time, it combines Gothic and
Renaissance elements with a unique charm.
Inside the church is a monument to Jean-
Baptiste Colbert (1619–1683), the finance
minister of Louis XIV. It was created by Antoine
Coysevox based on a design by Le Brun.

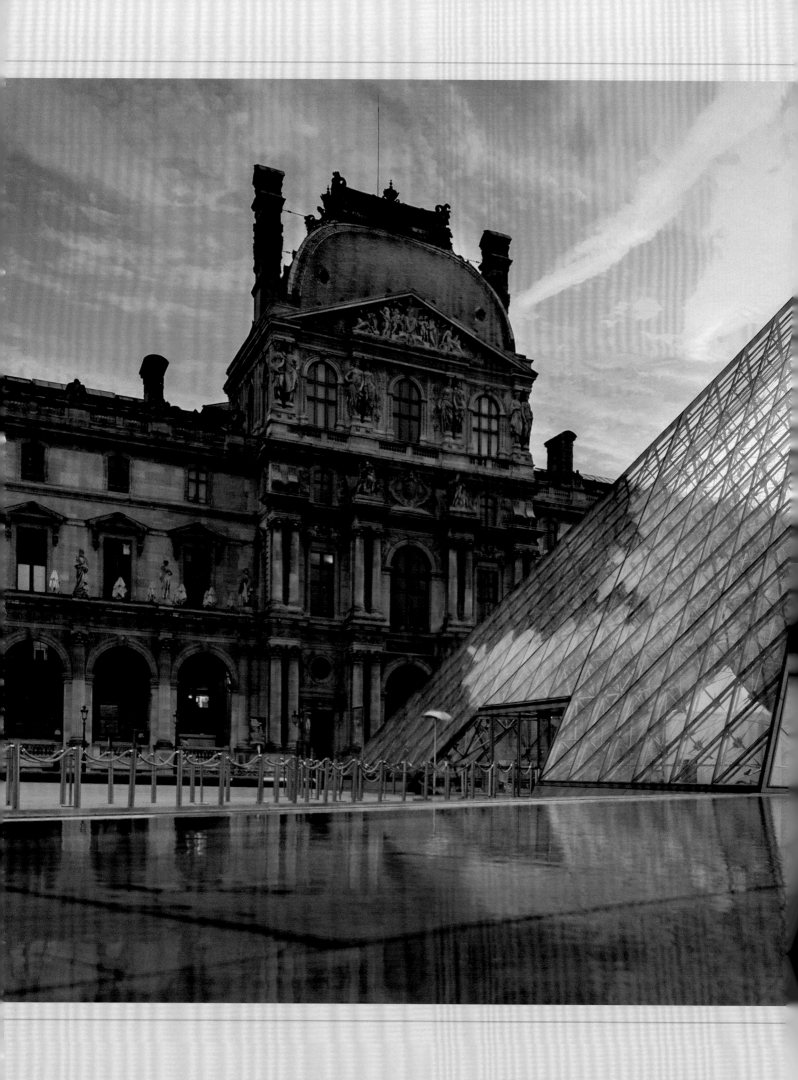

# LE LOUVRE

What is today probably the most famous museum in the world was originally built towards the end of the 12th century as a royal fortress. It was expanded on several occasions and served as the monarch's residence starting in the Renaissance up until the court moved to Versailles. It then fell into disrepair until it was revitalized as a museum during the Revolution in 1793. Major extensions, renovations and remodels with a more uniform, neo-classical style followed during the 19th and 20th centuries. In 1989, the spectacular glass pyramid was inaugurated. Designed by Ieoh Ming Pei, an American architect of Chinese origin, it is located between the massive wings of the building, Aile Denon and Aile Richelieu. Today, roughly 400,000 art treasures exhibited across more than 61,000 sq m (657,000 sq ft) of galleries attract over five million visitors every year.

# LE LOUVRE

For 800 years the Louvre was the residence of the French monarchy. It is said to be the second-largest palace in the world after the Vatican, but its current claim to fame is the museum it houses. The main entrance is marked by the glass pyramid erected in 1989 and designed by Ieoh Ming Pei. The foldout pages show the latter as well as the equestrian statue of Louis XIV, designed by Bernini.

# MASTERPIECES OF THE LOUVRE

The collections of the Louvre are divided into the departments of Egyptian antiquities, Oriental antiquities, Islamic art, Greek, Etruscan and Roman antiquities, crafts, sculptures, paintings, and drawings. Each of these departments presents masterpieces of the very highest quality, but despite this wealth of art treasures there are a number of very special works that we all associate with the museum. First and foremost is Leonardo da Vinci's *Mona Lisa*, whose much-publicized theft in 1911 contributed as much to the myth as her enigmatic smile. The *Venus de Milo* and the *Winged Victory of Samothrace*, two Greek statues of great classical beauty, are also here. The *Code of Hammurabi*, a stone engraved with one of the oldest collections of laws in the world, presides within these walls. Add to that the magnificent sculptures, frescoes and bas-reliefs in the Egyptian section, and treasures from ancient Greece and Italy. The sculpture department provides an overview of French works, and the most important paintings here include the *Pèlerinage à l'île de Cythère* (The Embarkation for Cythera) by Antoine Watteau, the "revolutionary" painting *La Liberté guidant le peuple* (Liberty leading the people) by Eugène Delacroix, and the *Medici cycle* by Rubens. Be sure to allow plenty of time for your visit!

The Louvre was to become a "museum for the people". That was the concept the revolutionary government had when they opened the museum to the public in 1793. Today, you can admire such masterpieces as *Winged Victory of Samothrace* (opposite page, far left), *Diana the Huntress* (below), or Goyay Lucientes *La Comtesse del Carpio*, far left) and Antoine Watteau's *Gilles* (left).

# THE SECRET OF THE MONA LISA

These days, the *Mona Lisa* smiles at her admirers from behind bulletproof glass, and there is a good reason for that. In 1911, Vincenzo Perugia stole the Da Vinci masterpiece because the Louvre had no alarm system. Two years later it reappeared, and since 1914 the world's most famous work of art still hangs in its original place, despite having survived further "attacks". *Mona Lisa* was apparently painted around 1503 or 1505, but the exact date is the subject of as much controversy as the identity of the person Da Vinci is portraying before his idealized landscape. Speculation that the portrait shows Lisa del Gioconda, wife of a wealthy Florentine merchant, can be traced back to Giorgio Vasari and would at least explain the painting's alternate name, *La Gioconda*. What is surprising is that Leonardo refused to part with the painting until shortly before he died, and only then did he sell it to King François I. After the Revolution, it was transferred to the Louvre. However, it is the *Mona Lisa* herself who appears to keep the biggest secret to herself: her smile. In the portrait, the artist dispensed with the usual creases around the eyes, often added to create the impression that the person is smiling. Instead he added shadows around the corner of the lady's mouth and gave her a suggestion of a squint.

# THE SECRET OF THE MONA LISA

*Mona Lisa*: Leonardo's portrait in oil on a very small, thin panel of poplar wood measures only 77 x 53 cm (29 x 21 in), but the stream of visitors at the Louvre is massive (below). Vincenzo Perugia, who stole the painting in 1911, said his motives were patriotic: he wanted to return the *Mona Lisa* to Italy. Italian officials saw things differently, however, and in December 1913 they returned her to her rightful owner (left).

# JARDIN DES TUILERIES

When people refer to the Tuileries today, they mean the Jardin des Tuileries – the palais of the same name was destroyed during the Paris Commune uprising of 1871. The palace was commissioned by Catherine de Medici in the mid-16th century, and for several centuries it was a city residence for the kings of France. The name "Tuileries" refers to the brick factory originally located here, but now the gardens between Place de la Concorde and the Louvre provide visitors with a relaxing place to stroll, sit beside the pond, or admire the statues by Aristide Maillol. Two museums flank the Tuileries: the Jeu de Paume towards the Rue de Rivoli (formerly the Impressionist museum, now an exhibition space for photography and video art), and the Orangerie, towards the Seine. The highlights in the Musée de l'Orangerie are the *Nymphéas* (Water Lilies) by Claude Monet.

In 1981, when the Louvre was transformed into the "Grand Louvre", the world's largest museum, on the orders of President François Mitterrand, the decision was also taken to give the neglected Tuileries a facelift. During the renovations, architects Wirtz, Cribier and Benech kept the original design from the gardens laid out by Le Nôtre, who was court gardener in the 17th century.

# MUSÉE DES ARTS DÉCORATIFS

As a result of the World Expos at the end of the 19th century, the opinion gradually gained currency that everyday objects could also have an artistic draw. In Paris, this concept resulted in the formation of the Union centrale des Arts décoratifs, an association for applied art that is known today as Les Arts Décoratifs. Since 1905, the association has been responsible for the Museum of Decorative Arts in the Marsan Wing of the Louvre. The exhibits included over 150,000 utensils and decorative items, from the Middle Ages to the present day. The main emphasis is on those styles regarded as being "typically French": Empire, Art Nouveau and Art Déco. The museum was re-opened after renovations in 2006, and is particularly proud of the valuable gold and jewelry work that it possesses. It also shows exhibits from other cultural spheres in its Islamic and Oriental departments.

After all the doorways and window openings were cleared, and the careful restoration of both the artworks and the building was completed in 2006, many of the 6,000 pieces in the museum saw daylight for the first time. The exhibits include Gerard Deschamps' *Pneumostructures* (far left), water toys that guarantee artistic rather than aquatic pleasures.

# RUE DE RIVOLI

One of the loveliest streets in the city stretches for more than three kilometers from Place de la Concorde, along the Jardin des Tuileries and the North Wing of the Louvre, then past the Place de l'Hôtel de Ville. The name of the Rue de Rivoli recalls the victory of Napoleon's army over Austria at Rivoli, Italy, in 1797. It was built in a homogenous architectural style during the first decades of the 19th century and was soon after linked to the Place de la Bastille via the Rue St-Antoine. Cafés, souvenir shops and traditional department stores, especially the Belle Jardinière and the Bazar de l'Hôtel de Ville, lure visitors to linger for a while. A popular motif for souvenir photos is the golden equestrian statue of Joan of Arc on the Place des Pyramides. It was created in 1874 by sculptor Emmanuel Frémiet.

"If it is the will of heaven that I return from this battle to a death crowned with victory, my work will be done," proclaims Schiller's *Maid of Orleans*. The equestrian statue of the French heroine on the Place des Pyramides (below) was created in 1899 by Emmanuel Frémiet and recalls her deeds. In the luxury hotel Le Meurice (left) visitors feel as if they have been transported back to the times of Louis XIV.

# PALAIS ROYAL

Anyone who is able to, typically invests in property at some point. Well, in the 17th century it was no different. In 1624, after just being appointed First Minister in the Council of State, the successful statesman and cardinal Armand-Jean du Plessis, Duke of Richelieu, purchased a plot of land near the Louvre. Five years later he was the proud resident of an elegant city palace, the Palais Cardinal, built by architect Jacques Lemercier. Just before his death in 1642, Richelieu left his impressive property to the king, Louis XIII, whereupon it became the Palais Royal, the largest royal palace after the Louvre. For several generations the elegant building remained in the possession of the royal family; Anne of Austria and her son Louis XIV also lived here. Today, the main building of the Palais Royal houses the Council of State and the French Ministry of Culture.

In 1780, the Palais Royal passed to Louis Philippe of Orléans, brother of Louis XIV, who then had the building extended on three sides towards the garden. During the 20th century, famous people lived in these apartments including writer Colette, the first woman in France to be accorded the honor of a state funeral. Art by Pol Bury (left) and Daniel Burens (below) now adorns the inner courtyard.

# THE MÉTRO: AN EXCURSION INTO THE PARIS UNDERWORLD

The first underground lines in Paris went into service in 1900, the year of the World Exposition: Line 1, from Porte de Vincennes to Porte Maillot, and Line 2, from Étoile to Trocadéro and Étoile to Porte Dauphine. Further sections were added during the years that followed. The first lines were completed under the direction of engineer Fulgence Marie Auguste Bienvenüe, after whom one of the metro stations is named (Montparnasse-Bienvenüe). The recognizable station entrances, with their stylish cast-iron frames and prominent Métro signs in Art-Nouveau fonts were designed by Hector Guimard. Today, the network covers sixteen lines with a total length of about 200 km (125 mi). Extensions are being planned as well. Added to that are the five lines of the RER (Réseau Express Régional), a sort of suburban train network that links the capital, for example, with the airport at Roissy and Disney Paris. The trains run between 5:00 a.m. and 00:30 a.m., and are typically able to bring passengers relatively close to their destinations: it is claimed that nowhere in Paris are you further than 500 m (550 yds) from the nearest metro station. However, visitors are recommended to avoid the daily rush hour, during which commuters from the suburbs flock into the city and return home again in the evening.

# THE MÉTRO: AN EXCURSION INTO THE PARIS UNDERWORLD

The sign bearing the name "Métropolitain" within a cast-iron frame, for example here at the station "Saint-Michel" (large photo), recall the beginnings of the Paris subway. Today, many stations have modern designs, while others are relatively plain . Others still, like the Concorde (bottom) and the Musée des Arts et Métiers (below), have been designed with references to their location.

# BANQUE DE FRANCE, PLACE DES VICTOIRES

With Place des Vosges, Place Dauphine, Place Vendôme and Place de la Concorde, the Place des Victoires is one of the five "royal squares" laid out during the 17th and 18th centuries. The design of the round plaza was the work of Jules Hardouin-Mansart; its magnificent surrounding buildings now house the stores of numerous luxury fashion brands. The equestrian statue of Louis XIV in the middle of the square was created by François Joseph Bosio and erected in 1810 to replace the monument destroyed during the Revolution. South of the square stands the monumental building of the Banque de France. Founded in 1800, on orders from Emperor Napoleon and initially subject to the laws governing private banks, the financial institution was nationalized in 1936, a status that lasted until deregulation in 1993. Today, it is one of Europe's leading banks.

Today, the blue, white and red tricolore and the European flag flutter above the Banque de France (below, the neoclassical entrance on the Rue de la Vrillière). The handsome building blends in effortlessly with the harmonious architectural ensemble of the Place des Victoires and the equestrian statue of King Louis XIV in the center (left).

Collecting books and manuscripts has a long tradition in France. Charles V (1364–1380, known as the Wise), for example, had an impressive library with one thousand volumes. In 1537, François I issued the "Ordonnance de Montpellier", decreeing that one copy of every printed book must be kept. The legislation formed the basis for the initial collection at the French National Library, which grows today by some 130,000 books annually. Since the 16th century, it has been steadily expanded to include engravings and etchings, prints, posters, music and photographs as well as audio equipment of all kinds, films and even online resources. The current stock includes some thirty million books and documents; since 1996, about one-third of them have been stored in the modern glass palaces on the Quai Bercy, while the rest are here in the "old" Bibliothèque Nationale in the Rue de Richelieu.

The National Library, on the Rue de Richelieu, was begun in 1645 by François Mansart and extended during the 18th century to include two galleries by Robert de Cotte. It is a mecca for booklovers, with domes supported by iron pillars spanning the halls like canopies. The window embrasures let daylight into the reading room, designed by Henri Labrouste in 1854.

# PALAIS DE LA BOURSE/PALAIS BRONGNIART

The Paris Stock Exchange has existed in some form or another since 1724. Initially it was housed in the Hôtel de Nevers, but in 1808, Napoleon laid the foundation stone for the neoclassical Palais de la Bourse. Designed by Alexandre Théodore Brongniart, the building is also known as the Palais Brongniart. After the architect's death, Eloi Labarre took over the task of completing the project. In 1903, the two side wings were added, and they match the main building perfectly in terms of style. Floor trading took place here from 1826, but lost importance in the 1990s as a result of the computer age. Now the building is used for events of all kinds, from receptions and conferences to seminars. The magnificent ambience of the interior is heightened by the elaborate ceiling paintings by historical painter Alexandre Abel de Pujol.

# PALAIS DE LA BOURSE/PALAIS BRONGNIART

Bull and bear markets are the financial world's terms to describe the rise and fall of stocks. When the main hall of the Palais de la Bourse was still active, visitors could still watch the floor trading from the gallery around the perimeter. The Corinthian pillars on the main façade recall temples from antiquity; the four statues symbolize justice, trade, agriculture and industry.

# PLACE VENDÔME

Place Vendôme, commissioned by Louis XIV and designed by architect Jules Hardouin-Mansart, is still the domain of the rich and beautiful. A number of famous international jewelers have their shops here, and the Grand Hotel Ritz is an establishment of world-renowned luxury. Ernest Hemingway felt so at home in the hotel's "Bar Américain" that he apparently said he hoped heaven would be as inviting. Frédéric Chopin may have been wondering the same thing when he died in Room 12 in 1849. There was once an equestrian statue of the "Sun King" here, just like on Place des Victoires, but it was removed in 1792 during the Revolution. From 1810, the view was of a column surmounted by a statue of Napoleon and built in the style of Trajan's Column in Rome. In 1870, the column was toppled by revolutionaries but was put back in its place three years later.

In the sea of lights at night on the Place Vendôme you will feel as if you have been taken back in time. The square owes its name to the Duc de Vendôme, an illegitimate son of Henry IV and Gabrielle d'Estrées, whose residence stood here. The Hotel Ritz is an institution that hit the headlines when Princess Diana set off from here on her fatal car journey in 1997.

# DIAMONDS ARE A GIRL'S BEST FRIEND

Most people have to restrict their activities on Place Vendôme to window shopping – this is where the most expensive and exclusive jewelers in the world can be found. Indeed, the fine jewelry and expensive watches here have been luring lovers of beautiful and precious things for more than one hundred years to this harmoniously designed square in the First Arrondissement. The French refer to jewelry shops in this segment as haute joaillierie, like haute couture or haut cuisine. Back in 1893, Frédéric Boucheron was the first of the famous jewelers to establish his shop in the Place Vendôme, followed soon afterwards by Louis François Cartier (1898), Joseph Chaumet (1902) and Alfred van Cleef & Solomon Arpels (1906). Then, in the 20th century, more famous shops were added such as Fred, Mauboussin and Bulgari, as well as exclusive watches including Patek Philippe, Rolex and Piaget. If you wish to display your expensive new purchases in the right setting, you will find the perfect opportunity to do so in the restaurant at the Hotel Ritz next door. Let's face it, what could be finer than sipping a glass of champagne in the bar, with the newly acquired diamonds twinkling on your ears, competing for attention with the pearly bubbles tinkling in the glass?

# DIAMONDS ARE A GIRL'S BEST FRIEND

The oldest jewelry shop on the square is Boucheron (left and bottom). Founded in 1858, it moved into its present location on Place Vendôme in 1893. Despite its sense of tradition, the company also has a feeling for contemporary trends; British star designer Alexander McQueen (1969–2010) designed jewelry for Boucheron. Fred (other photos) is the first name of its founder Fred Samuel.

# LA MADELEINE

If you walk along Rue Royale from Place de la Concorde, you may not believe your eyes: why is there a Greek temple in the center of Paris? It was an order from Louis XV (1715–1774) that architect Contant d'Ivryan begin a church on this spot in 1764. After the architect's death in 1777, his colleague Guillaume-Martin Couture took over supervision of the project, changing the plans to follow a different model, the Pantheon. Progress was slow and the building was far from completed when work had to stop in 1790, and did not continue until the Revolution was over. It was not until sixteen years later, in 1806, that Napoleon had new plans drawn up – initially for a Temple of Fame. Then he changed his mind: it was to become a (parish) church after all. However, the building was not consecrated until 1845, almost a quarter of a century after Napoleon's death in 1821.

The colonnade around the building is more reminiscent of an ancient temple than a church: fifty-two Corinthian columns, each 20 m (65 ft) high, support a frieze decorated with sculptures. The pediment is adorned with a relief of the Last Judgement by Philippe Lemaire, and the high altar inside the church contains a group of statues by sculptor Carlo Marochetti, who was born in Turin but grew up in Paris.

# FAUCHON

For gourmets planning to not just indulge their passion for food in the restaurants of the French capital, but also hoping to take some of the rare delicacies home with them, 26 Place Madeleine is an absolute top address. For more than a century, this has been the location of Fauchon, the leading delicatessen in France – if not the world. Auguste Fauchon founded the firm in 1886, and before long experienced great success thanks to the high-quality products he offered. Since 1905, foodies have no longer actually had to travel to France to shop at Fauchon, as they can select and order the items from a catalogue at home. Still, the pleasure of enjoying the delicacies on-location in the first Salon de Thé, founded in 1888, is a much better experience. Today, there is even a caviar bar at Place de la Madeleine.

Fauchon, at Place de la Madeleine, is a famous pilgrimage destination for gourmets from all over the world. The elegant ambience underlines the exclusivity and high quality of the products on sale here. Apart from tea – it was here that the first major selection of aromatized black tea was created in the 1960s – one of the most popular delights at Fauchon is the caviar.

# OPÉRA GARNIER

Opera in Paris was born in 1669, when Louis XIV commissioned poet and librettist Pierre Perrin with the establishment of a royal music academy, primarily to enable opera performances. In the 200 years that followed, the academy changed locations a number of times, until Napoleon III hired the more or less unknown, 35-year-old architect Charles Garnier to build a new venue that would finally serve as the institution's permanent location. Construction began two years later, but they hit groundwater in the process and were forced to build a large basin, which created the dome that now supports the building. This subterranean "lake" was of course the inspiration for Gaston Leroux's *Phantom of the Opera*, which was later made into a successful musical by Andrew Lloyd Webber. The opera house was first opened in 1875, with much fanfare.

# OPÉRA GARNIER

Since the opening of the Opéra Bastille in 1989, the Opéra Garnier, where Maria Callas last took the stage in 1965 as the lead in Bellini's Norma, has mostly been used for ballet performances. Still, the building on the Place de l'Opéra, which was conceived as a traffic hub by city prefect Baron Haussmann, is a stunning sight. The interior features a spectacular staircase as well as ceiling frescoes from Chagall from 1963.

# NAPOLEON III, BARON HAUSSMANN AND THE REDEVELOPMENT OF PARIS

The plans drafted by Emperor Napoleon III made a very important contribution to the more recent architectural history of Paris. Together with the prefect of the city at that time, Georges Eugène Baron Haussmann (1809–1891), he planned a wide-ranging and fundamental modernization of the capital, which was still largely medieval with regard to both its buildings and its layout. Paris was to become a city that could stand comparison with the other European capitals like London, Vienna and Berlin. Napoleon III was also motivated by strategic considerations. Along the broad, straight roads it would be more difficult to defend against potential attacks by revolutionaries. The memories of battles at the barricades in Paris' streets during the uprisings of 1830 and 1848 were indeed still vivid. The famous Grands Boulevards – the Rue de Rivoli, the area around the Opéra Garnier, and the roads converging on the Arc de Triomphe – are all the work of Haussmann, or at least they clearly bear his stamp. And the neoclassical buildings that seem to us today to be so typical of Paris, were also built during this period. Haussmann's forward-looking designs created spacious streets that are still able to cope with the traffic of the modern metropolis.

# NAPOLEON III, BARON HAUSSMANN AND THE REDEVELOPMENT OF PARIS

Left: The emperor and his prefect. "... everywhere, vistas are opening up. Paris is being hacked apart as with the strokes of a saber, and its arteries have been opened to feed hundreds of thousands of workers and bricklayers. Finally, the city will be traversed by strategic axes that will make us gaze in awe and allow us to transfer mighty powers to the very heart of the old city districts." (Émile Zola)

# PRINTEMPS

Visitors strolling along Boulevard Haussmann will be faced with a difficult choice between the two big Paris department stores: Printemps and Galeries Lafayette. Erected in 1865 as "Grands Magasins du Printemps", the shopping temple now consists of four buildings, two of which are on the adjacent Rue de Provence: Printemps de la Mode (fashion), Printemps de la Beauté et de la Maison (cosmetics and home), Printemps de l'Homme (men's fashion) and Citadium (trendy, urban fashion). There are also a number of places to eat and drink, from relaxed cafés to high-end restaurants, two of which are particularly distinctive: the Brasserie Printemps, under the Art-Nouveau glass dome from 1924, and the self-service restaurant Déli-cieux (délicieux = delicious, cieux = heaven), on the ninth floor roof terrace with a panorama of the Sacré-Cœur and the Eiffel Tower.

These magnificent, 19th-century department
store buildings feature fantastic interior
architecture. Decorative details such as the
Art-Nouveau dome of colored glass make this
already unique shopping experience that much
more enjoyable alongside the elegant fashions
and wide range of cosmetics here.

# GALERIES LAFAYETTE

The Galeries Lafayette is one of the most famous department store in the world, with a number of branches in France and abroad. It opened in 1894, with its close neighbor and competitor, Printemps, opening thirty years later. Since 1912, the main store has been in the magnificent building on Boulevard Haussmann, near the Havre-Caumartin métro, and just a stone's throw from the Opéra Garnier. The main focus at the beginning was women's fashion, whereas today you will also find men's fashion, cosmetics, toys and fine china on a sales area of 70,000 sq m (72 ha). The demographics of the clientele has also changed over the years: of the 100,000 or so customers who come here every day, the Chinese are now the largest group among foreigners, followed by the Americans and the Japanese.

The main hall of the flagship store on Boulevard Haussmann is an impressive sight, several storeys high and topped by a magnificent Art-Nouveau dome decorated with stained glass. At Christmas, the Galeries Lafayette shines with a seasonal lighting ensemble. The roof terrace here affords magnificent panoramic views of the city.

# PARIS ARCADES: "A STROLL THROUGH THE LIVING ROOM"

Arcades seem to be a Parisian invention: passageways with glass roofs linking two bustling streets and giving visitors the option of a pleasant stroll, sheltered from the wind and weather. Philosopher Walter Benjamin was right when he described the Paris arcades, which became fashionable in the 1820s, as "living rooms for strolling". Their predecessors were the arcades along the Rue de Rivoli and by the Palais Royal, but they were later super-seded by the "Grands Magasins", the department stores. Today, the Paris arcade concept has been revived inside modern metropolitan shopping centers. Often described as "galleries", they are still designed to lure visitors with the appearance of a pleasant stroll, during which shoppers will use the comfortable environment to spend a bit of money. The most magnificent example of a Parisian (shopping) arcade is the Galerie Véro-Dodat in the 1st ar-rondissement, built by two butchers in 1826. Also worth a visit, in the 2nd arrondissement, are the Galerie Vivienne (1823), the Passage des Panoramas with its coffered ceiling, the Galerie Colbert (1826) with the Jean-Paul Gaultier perfumery, and the Galerie Grand Cerf with a 12-m-high (39-ft) glass roof. In the 9th arrondissement, visitors flock to the Passage Verdeau (1847) and the Passage Jouffroy, which had underfloor heating as early as 1847.

# PARIS ARCADES: "A STROLL THROUGH THE LIVING ROOM"

The arcades of Paris could also be described, rather dramatically, as "allegories of temptation and seductiveness, with sophisticated (often dim) lighting and an exclusive atmosphere". There were once over 100 of them. Today, you can stroll in the Passage Jouffroy (left), or stay in the Hôtel Chopin. In the Passage Verdeau (below left and right) you will be tempted by the rare items and antiques.

# FAUBOURG SAINT-HONORÉ

The Faubourg Saint-Honoré district derives its name from the eponymous street that runs through it for several kilometers: Rue du Faubourg Saint-Honoré, which starts at Place des Ternes and runs east toward Les Halles (parallel with Pont Neuf). The fact that there is no house with the number 13 is due to the superstitious Empress Eugénie, wife of Napoleon III, who had the number removed. That does not detract from the exclusivity of the neighborhood, however: the Presidential Palace, the Ministry of the Interior and many international embassies are all grouped close to each other on the Rue du Faubourg Saint-Honoré, as are the headquarters of renowned fashion houses, which surely benefit from having a presence on the block. They include couturiers such as Pierre Cardin, Louis Féraud, Hermès, Karl Lagerfeld, Jeanne Lanvin and Yves Saint-Laurent.

If you walk along the famous Rue Faubourg Saint-Honoré, you will find a shopping temptation at practically every corner. Especially during the pre-Christmas period, when the shop windows and rows of houses are festively lit and lavishly decorated (bottom left), visitors are drawn to the shops like moths to the light. Top, left to right: Hermès and Gucci; below right: Prada's Miu Miu line.

# TRÈS CHIC: PARIS FASHION

Despite increasing competition from London, Milan and New York, Paris is still the focal point of haute couture. The term, in its current form, originated here, and even if it was an Englishman, Charles Frederick Worth, who established the first house of haute couture in Paris, in 1858, the rich and beautiful were willing to pay generously to be among his clientele. One of Worth's assistants, Paul Poiret, went on to become a world-famous designer himself. After World War II, haute couture became more accessible through the New Look, a movement created by Christian Dior that was then copied by many companies. In the late 1940s, prêt-à-porter (ready-to-wear clothes, not exclusive, one-off pieces) appeared on the scene, adding a second string to the bows of many couture houses. Fashion was now available to a larger – though admittedly still affluent – clientele. To be considered part of Parisian haute couture, a couturier must present a collection twice a year, comprising at least thirty-five "runs", and have at least fifteen full-time employees. The reputation of Paris as the world's fashion capital is maintained by such names as Chanel, Dior, Givenchy, Ungaro, Gaultier, Lacroix and Valentino. To learn more about French fashion, visit the Musée de la Mode et du Costume de la Ville de Paris.

Twice a year, in spring and fall, Paris' fashion world celebrates the industry's most important event, Paris Fashion Week. Sweeping the catwalks here are haute-couture creations by Givenchy (left) and Chanel, staged by fashion houses such as Jean-Paul Gaultier, Yves Saint-Laurent and Christian Lacroix.

# PALAIS DE L'ÉLYSÉE

The Palais de Élysée is named after the nearby Champs-Élysées, but only the garden side faces the grand boulevard. The main façade, commissioned by the Count of Évreux in 1718, looks out over Rue du Faubourg Saint-Honoré. After the count's death, King Louis XV bought it for his mistress, the Marquise de Pompadour. It later belonged to Napoleon, who signed his second, and final deed of abdication here in 1815, after losing the Battle of Waterloo in Belgium. Since 1873, it has been the seat of the French president, who, constitutionally, is not only responsible for the representative duties customary in parliamentary systems, but also possesses such wide-ranging political powers that his position nearly echoes that of a monarch. Looking at it that way, perhaps the Élysée Palace is just grand enough to serve as the official residence of the French head of state...

Since Charles de Gaulle – who played a major role in formulating the constitution of the Fifth Republic – all of the French presidents have adopted the role as head of state, a position eerily reminiscent to that of a monarch. Once you see the interior of the government palace you will understand why presidents in office have to endure allusions to Louis XIV, who was known as the "Sun King".

# GRAND PALAIS

Between the Champs-Élysées and the Seine are two impressive buildings with glass roofs supported by steel frames: the Grand Palais and the Petit Palais. They were both built for the 1900 World Expo as part of a town-planning project aimed at creating a visual axis between the grand boulevard and the Dôme des Invalides. Three architects were involved in the building of the Grand Palais, in which important art exhibitions are still held: Henri-Adolphe-Auguste Deglane was responsible for the façade overlooking Avenue Winston Churchill and the great glazed hall; Albert-Félix-Théophile Thomas was responsible for the part facing the Avenue Franklin D. Roosevelt; and Louis-Albert Louvet was responsible for the central section and the main staircase. The work was coordinated by Charles Giraut, who was also charged with the construction of the Petit Palais.

The inscription above the west entrance of the Grand Pavillon is dedicated to "The glory of French art". The bronze quadriga above the side pavilion was the work of Georges Récipon. The dome structure is particularly impressive: it is 45 m (150 ft) high and constructed of steel and iron. Since 1937, the west wing has been home to the "Palace of Discovery", a museum of science.

# PETIT PALAIS

Charles Girault built the Petit Palais at the same time as the Grand Palais – during the 1900 World Exposition – with the purpose of presenting a retrospective of French art. Since the interior of the building was only to be illuminated with natural light, Girault ensured that all sides of the building would allow plenty of it to come in from outside. Two years after the Expo, the trapezoidal complex, with its two galleries grouped in a semi-circular garden, was remodeled as the home of the Museum of Fine Arts of the City of Paris. Its art collection, largely consisting of donations, today exhibits some 1,300 paintings, sculptures, tapestries, objets d'art and icons, from antiquity to the beginning of the 20th century. Highlights include works by Delacroix, Monet, Sisley, Renoir, Toulouse-Lautrec and Courbet.

The Petit Palais, Paris' largest municipal museum, also underwent major renovations (2001–2005), during which the glass façade of the gallery was once again opened to the Cours de la Reine. No less interesting than the collections here are the architecture and furnishings of the museum building itself – an artwork in its own right.

# PONT ALEXANDRE III

The Pont Alexandre III bridge was also built in conjunction with the 1900 World Expo, with the intention of creating a direct link, called for by the city-planners, between the Avenue des Champs-Élysées and the Dôme des Invalides on about the level of the Grand Palais and the Petit Palais. Russian Czar Nicholas II, son of Czar Alexander III, with whom France had signed a treaty in 1892, and after whom the bridge is named, laid the foundation stone on October 7, 1896. It was then unveiled by Emile Loubet on opening day of the 1900 World Expo. Designed by engineer Jean Résal, it is regarded as a masterpiece of bridge architecture. At its four corners are monumental pillars 17 m (56 ft) in height and topped by gilt bronze figures, each accompanied by a winged Pegasus; they are meant to symbolize the glory of science, art, trade and industry.

This bridge is over 100 m (330 ft) long and 40 m (132 ft) wide, spanning the river without supporting pillars in one elegant steel arch. It is decorated with candelabras and garlands. Two hammered copper allegories show the nymphs of the Seine on the upstream side, and the nymphs of the Neva on the downstream side (below). In the evening, thirty-two lanterns bathe the bridge in atmospheric light (left).

PLACE DE LA CONCORDE

# PLACE DE LA CONCORDE

If you walk down the Champs-Élysées, your gaze will eventually focus, even from a distance, on the 22-m-high (75-ft) pink granite obelisks flanked by two fountains that once stood in Luxor, Egypt, but since 1833 have marked the center of the Place de la Concorde. The octagonal plaza, which is adjacent to the Jardin des Tuileries, is the largest of its kind in Paris. It was planned between 1755 and 1775 by Jacques-Ange Gabri-

el, who also designed the two temple-like buildings on the north side that house the Naval Ministry and the Hotel Crillon. The square was originally named after King Louis XV, but in 1793, when his grandson Louis XVI was sent to the guillotine here – with his wife Marie-Antoinette – the bloody plaza was renamed "Place de la Révolution". Two years later it was given its current, slightly less historically charged name.

Architect Jakob Ignaz Hittorf, a native of Cologne, gave the Place de la Concorde its current appearance under "bourgeois King" Louis Philippe I (1830–1848). The center of the square is marked by an obelisk that is over 3,000 years old and once stood in front of the temple of Ramses II in Thebes. It is now flanked by two bronze fountains: the Fontaine des Mers (left) and the Fontaine des Fleuves.

# AVENUE DES CHAMPS-ÉLYSÉES, ARC DE TRIOMPHE

The Avenue des Champs-Élysées is one of the world's most famous streets. A grand military parade takes place each year here on July 14, "Bastille Day". Spectators cheer cyclists to the finish line here during the Tour de France, and Parisians and visitors from around the world welcome in the New Year here. But on any given day, the stretch of road between Place de la Concorde and Place Charles de Gaulle is busy with traffic and pedestrians. The Arc de Triomphe stands strong as cars whirl around it and a dozen roads radiate from it to form a star shape – the reason it was called Place de l'Étoile until 1969. Completed in 1836, the monumental arch is a memorial to Emperor Napoleon's victories. In the shadow of this symbolic monument, the flame on the Tomb of the Unknown Soldier flickers in remembrance.

Shops, offices, banks and theaters alternate on both sides of the Champs-Élysées (left). The north-west end of the grand boulevard is marked by the Arc de Triomphe, begun in 1806 based on designs by Jean-François Chalgrin. The arch is 50 m (495 ft) high and 40 m (132 ft) wide and was not finished for thirty years – after Napoleon I was already gone.

# PALAIS DE CHAILLOT, JARDINS DU TROCADÉRO

The Palais de Chaillot was built for the 1937 World Exposition on the site of the Trocadéro, a fanciful building that had previously been erected for the 1878 World Exposition and named after a Spanish fortress that had been conquered in 1823. The Palais houses three museums: the Museum of Architecture in the East Wing, the Museum of Ethnology and the Maritime Museum in the West Wing. In the basement of the palais you will find the famous Théâtre National de Chaillot, with two auditoriums and a small studio theater. Beneath the complex, which is on a hill, is the Jardins du Trocadéro, a park that was also laid out for the 1937 World Expo. Like the terrace of the Palais de Chaillot, from which you have the best view of the Eiffel Tower, the gardens are a popular meeting place for Parisians and their guests from all over the world.

# PALAIS DE CHAILLOT, JARDINS DU TROCADÉRO

Not many people take note of the fact that the monumental architecture of the Palais de Chaillot is derived from the ideals of the time in which it was built. During the 1937 World Fair, the German and Soviet pavilions faced each other here. The square between the two wings of the complex represents an ideal corrective to the Fascist architecture: since 1987, it has been known as the "Square of Human Rights".

# PALAIS DE TOKYO/MUSÉE D'ART MODERNE DE LA VILLE DE PARIS (MAM)

Like the nearby Palais de Chaillot, the Palais de Tokyo was built for the 1937 World Expo. Since 1961, it has housed the Musée d'Art Moderne de la Ville de Paris, whose collections include important works such as *La Danse* by Henri Matisse and the enormous *La Fée Électricité* by Raoul Dufy. The study of art from the modern age, in all its facets, is a pleasurable occupation that finds an ideal setting in many places in Paris, most of all here. Rotating exhibitions in all areas of contemporary art (painting, graphics, sculpture, photography, video, design, fashion, dance) can be found in the Institution Palais de Tokyo / Site de Création Contemporaine, which was established in 2002. Here, art extends beyond the exhibition area itself: the floor of the restaurant is decorated with a work by artist Michael Lin.

# PALAIS DE TOKYO/MUSÉE D'ART MODERNE DE LA VILLE DE PARIS (MAM)

The Municipal Museum of Modern Art exhibits its works in chronological order (below: a piece by Matthew Ritchie), from the beginnings of Classical Modernism in the 20th century (Fauvism, Cubism) to contemporary art. Below: The works of art at the Palais de Tokyo also inspire young visitors. Above: The entrance of the palace is decorated with a sculpture of reclining nymphs; the works of Lucio Fontana.

# RIVE GAUCHE

The name of the Quartier Latin ("Latin Quarter") dates from the time when the Sorbonne, France's oldest university, was founded in Paris and Latin was still regarded as the language of scholars. Student life still defines this lively neighborhood, with its countless bookshops, restaurants, cinemas and clubs. Faubourg Saint-Germain, another district that also lies on the Left Bank (the southern bank of the Seine) is comparatively tranquil but boasts a number of fine museums. The Left Bank is also home to perhaps Paris' most famous icon: the Eiffel Tower.

Three sights in one picture: the Panthéon,
ecalling personalities like Clovis I, who in 508
made Paris the capital of his Kingdom of the
Franks; the Tour Montparnasse rising skyward
on its own; and the Eiffel Tower, another solitary
masterpiece.

# JARDIN DES PLANTES

Even royalty occasionally suffer from aches and pains. In order to relieve the complaints of King Louis XIII (1610–1643), his personal doctors planted an herb garden with medicinal plants. Under botanist Georges Buffon (1707–1788), the garden was expanded into a magnificent park – though it had been open to the public from 1640. During the Revolution, Parisians for the first time were able to see the exotic animals brought here from Ver-sailles. The menagerie, built for this purpose in 1794, became the original stock of the zoo that still exists here. Housing was later built for the large mammals along with aviaries and greenhouses with characteristic steel-and-glass structures. An alpine garden, a rose garden and rare plants were introduced. The oldest "inhabitant" of the Botanical Garden is a *Robinia pseudoacacia* (Black Locust). It is said to have been planted in 1636.

Legend has it that, in 1734, botanist Bernard de Jussieu (1699–1777) smuggled two clippings of Lebanese cedars from England to Paris in his hat. In fact, he transported them in a planter pot, but the pot broke shortly before he reached his destination, which is where the hat part of the story comes in – and hence the legend. They can still be seen in the Botanical Garden.

# MUSÉUM NATIONAL D'HISTOIRE NATURELLE

The main branch of the National Museum for Natural History is also on the site of the Jardin des Plantes. Its first director, when it was founded back in 1793, was mineralogist Louis Jean-Marie Daubenton. The museum, which also doubles as a research institute, has numerous branches inside and outside Paris, and is one of the biggest of its kind today. The "Galerie de Minéralogie, de Géologie et de Paléobotanique" contains more than 600,000 rare minerals and meteorites, while the "Galerie de Paléontologie et d'Anatomie comparée" contains more than a million skeletons. A special attraction – not only for children – is the "Galerie de l'Evolution", built in 1889 by Jules André. In the middle stands a long procession of stuffed animals that visualize the history of the development of living things. Also on view are models of animals that are extinct today.

In the "Gallery of Evolution", at the National Museum of Natural History, it looks as if a caravan of antelopes, elephants, lions, rhinoceroses, zebras and other animals has gathered to make its way to Noah's Ark. Its many exhibits are an inspiring way to learn about the history of earth and its countless creatures.

# INSTITUT DU MONDE ARABE, MOSQUÉE DE PARIS

The Institut du Monde Arabe was founded in 1980 on the initiative of France and twenty Arab states. Its aim is to provide information about Arabic language and culture for those who are hesitant about establishing contact with the Islamic world, especially in these times of increasing migration. The intercultural understanding between the Orient and the Occident is based on mission and obligation, something that is evidenced by the exterior of the complex, which is home to a library, several lecture theaters, a museum and a documentation center. The team of architects, led by Jean Nouvel, aimed to create a synthesis of Western and Eastern architectural concepts, on the one hand, and bridge the gap between tradition and modernity, on the other. This also applies to the mosque, which is further to the south, donated by the City of Paris in 1920 and which also welcomes non-Muslims.

The southern façade of the Institut du Monde Arabe is clad with 240 panels, each one storey high. They form an electro-technical version of the traditionally wood lattice work that filter the sunlight in Arab-style houses. The frequently changing exhibitions inside are a constant source of interest. Left: The Paris Mosque, built between 1922 and 1926 in Spanish-Moorish style.

# THE SORBONNE: OVER 750 YEARS OF EUROPEAN INTELLECTUALISM

The history of the Sorbonne goes back to 1253, when Robert de Sorbon (1201–1274) founded the "Maison de Sorbonne", with the financial support of the king. Sorbon was canon of the cathedral and Louis IX's confessor, and had assumed the name of his native village in the Ardennes, hence the university's name. In his youth he had been a poor student, and his college for indigent students of theology soon became one of the most important centers of European intellectual life. Its graduates included Thomas Aquinas, Simone de Beauvoir, Marie Curie, Albertus Magnus and Claude-Lévi-Strauss. Only one chapel remains of the new building, created in the mid-17th century under Cardinal Richelieu. In the years 1885–1901, the Sorbonne was extended based on designs by Henri-Paul Nénot and became the biggest university in France. Closely linked with its name is the unrest of May 1968, during which students egged each other on with comments like "Be realistic, demand the impossible". Today, three independent universities (of thirteen in the city), share the name Sorbonne and the old complex of buildings in the Quartier Latin. They are known as Paris I Panthéon-Sorbonne, Paris III Sorbonne Nouvelle, and Paris IV Paris-Sorbonne and they were created during the university reform of 1970/71.

# THE SORBONNE: OVER 750 YEARS OF EUROPEAN INTELLECTUALISM

The oldest surviving building at the university is the university chapel, designed by Jacques Lemercier between 1635 and 1642 (left). The Grand Amphithéâtre is used for ceremonial occasions and provides space for 2,700 guests; the rooms of the library (below), paneled with fine wood, provide a suitably venerable home for the assembled volumes of eras gone by.

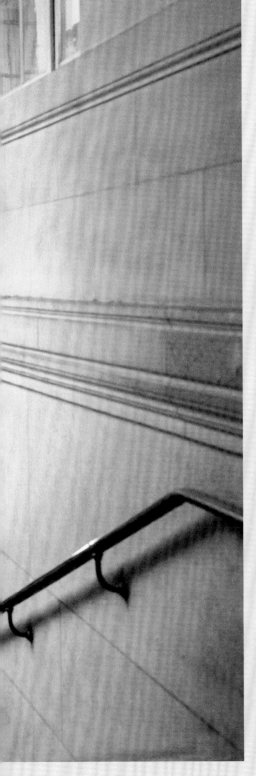

# PANTHÉON

In 1744, King Louis XIV, gravely ill, vowed that if he recovered he would build a new church in honor of St Genevieve, patron saint of Paris, on the highest spot on the left bank of the Seine. Indeed, when he was restored to health he decided to go big with his plans, commissioning the Marquis de Marigny, brother of Madame de Pompadour, to create a monument that would be the largest religious building of the 18th century. The foundation stone was laid in 1764, and the edifice itself was designed by Jacques-Germain Soufflot in the form of a Greek cross measuring a colossal 110 x 84 m (363 x 277 ft) with a height of 83 m (270 ft). Financial difficulties delayed its completion until 1790 – the year of the revolution. Thereafter, the building's purpose was changed several times, from a hall of fame to a church and then a memorial site, which it remains today.

"Panthéonisation" is the French term used when famous people are "moved" to the Pantheon, usually years after their death. Marie Curie was the first woman to end up here, albeit not until 1995 (she died in 1934). The president alone makes the decision. The building was sed by physicist Léon Foucault in 1851, when he sed the pendulum named after him to prove the rotation of the Earth.

# LITERATURE IN THE QUARTIER LATIN: SHAKESPEARE & COMPANY

"Shakespeare & Company" is a bookshop for more than just English-language literature. It is an institution in the cultural fabric of Paris. Sylvia Beach, who was born in Baltimore, Maryland, in 1887, and moved to Paris in 1901, opened the first shop with this name in 1919. It soon became a popular meeting place for the countless English-speaking writers in the metropolis on the Seine. Hemingway and Scott Fitzgerald read from their works in the Rue de l'Odéon, and James Joyce frequented the establishment. In 1922, Beach published Joyce's masterpiece *Ulysses*, which had previously been rejected by several publishers. When she died in 1962, George Whitman continued the tradition she had developed, renaming the bookshop he had founded in 1951, "Le Mistral", on Rue de la Bûcherie, to "Shakespeare & Company". Henry Miller, Allen Ginsberg and Anaïs Nin once discussed the latest trends in literature in this labyrinthine bookshop in the Quartier Latin, which sells second-hand rarities as well as the latest volumes. To this day, "Shakespeare & Company" is a venue for readings, and every two years it hosts the awards ceremony for the "Paris Literary Prize". It also has an unusual way of encouraging young writers: they are allowed to live for a while free of charge above the famous bookshop.

"Here, on a cold, windswept street, was a warm and cozy place in winter, with a big stove, and with tables and shelves full of books," wrote Ernest Hemingway about Sylvia Beach's bookshop "Shakespeare and Company", whose tradition was continued from 1951 by George Whitman. Since 2003, his daughter Sylvia has run this "Wonderland of books" (Henry Miller) on the left bank of the Seine.

# PALAIS DU LUXEMBOURG

It is quite some time since people claimed this building was haunted. If that were really to be the case, however, it would be the ghosts of parliamentarism that haunt it – for today this is the seat of the French Senate, the highest legislative body in the country apart from the National Assembly. At the beginning of the 13th century, it was a ruined castle, the Château Vauvert, where there were allegedly numerous ghosts. To put an end to the problem, King Louis IX (Saint Louis) declared that the site should be inhabited by Carthusian monks starting in 1257. They then prepared the way for Marie de Medici, who in 1612 purchased a city palais that had been built here in the meantime by the Duc de Luxembourg. She had it rebuilt to create today's palace and gradually transformed the surrounding land into a park.

After her husband Henry IV had been killed, Marie de Medici chose to leave the Louvre. As part of the interior decoration of her new residence, which had been designed by Salomon de Brosse, Rubens painted a twenty-four-part series glorifying her name – the "Medici Cycle". To admire it today, however, even members of parliament, who now meet n the Palais, have to go back to the Louvre.

# JARDIN DU LUXEMBOURG

Nobody can resist the charms of the largest and most beautiful public park in Paris, the Jardin du Luxembourg. In the words of historian and journalist Johannes Willms, "It is the setting for romantic trysts, while pensioners watch the voluptuous "bonnes" (nannies), who gather around the pond to gossip, with its big fountain in the main parterre, and the older children look after their model boats as they sail across the water."

All that is left nowadays of Catherine de Medici's old Baroque garden, which formed the historic heart of today's park, is the Fontaine Médici. The bronze and marble sculpture group represents an episode from classical mythology in which the jealous cyclops, Polyphemus, surprises his unexpecting mistress, Galatea, in a grotto with the young herd, Acis.

Since the old charterhouse of the Carthusian monks was demolished in 1790, the visual axis from the Palais du Luxembourg, in the middle of the park, extends as far as the Avenue de l'Observatoire. During the Revolution, famous prisoners were held here before they were led to the guillotine, but today, life in the park is comparatively relaxed and quite inviting.

# SAINT-SULPICE

The Abbey of St-Germain-des-Prés owed its prosperity mainly to the fields outside the monastery walls. Since the abbey church was reserved for the monks, a parish church was built in the 12th century for the workers. Its patron saint was Saint Sulpitius II (the Pious) of Bourges, the archbishop and spiritual advisor of the Merovingian king Chlothar II. The old Romanesque church of Saint-Sulpice was replaced by a new building in the 17th and 18th centuries; at first glance, its relatively homogeneous appearance conceals the fact that six architects were involved in its construction. The first designs were the work of Christophe Gamard, and the last architect who was involved was Giovanni Niccolò Servandoni, from Florence, who designed the main façade in 1732, with its twin towers of differing heights; the southern tower remained unfinished.

The impressive dimensions of the church are inspired by the floor plan of Notre-Dame; it is 118 m (390 ft) long and 57 m (188 ft) wide. Charles Baudelaire and the Marquis de Sade were both baptized here, and Heinrich Heine and Victor Hugo both held their weddings here. The biggest organ in France works its magic inside these walls, its casing having been designed in 1776 by Jean-François Chalgrin.

# EVERYTHING THE HEART DESIRES: PARIS MARKETS

Anyone who enjoys strolling through markets will find plenty of opportunities to do so in the French capital. In fact, each arrondissement offers a number of markets of different types on different days of the week. The biggest flower market in Paris, for example, is on the Île de la Cité, just a stone's throw from Notre-Dame. On Sundays, on the other hand, a variety of bird species are offered for sale here amidst the sea of flowers. There are of course food markets in most of the arrondissements; the one in Rue Mouffetard in the Quartier Latin is especially famous. The Marché Biologique, the organic food market on Boulevard Raspail (Métro Notre-Dame-des-Champs) is popular particularly on Sundays as a place to stroll and buy fresh groceries. There are also organic food markets at Place Louis-Lépine (Métro Cité) and in Cour Marigny (Métro Champs-Élysées). Below the Bar-bès-Rochechouart métro station, visitors can immerse themselves in an "exotic" world: in the surrounding Goutte d'Or district, many of the residents are of Arab and African descent, and the wide range of products tends to suit their needs and preferences. The most popular flea market, the "Marché aux Puces" at Saint-Ouen, lies on the outskirts of Paris, but the atmosphere is calmer among the junk dealers at Place d'Aligre.

The range of goods on the markets is vast and recalls Émile Zola's legendary *Le Ventre de Paris* (The Belly of Paris): "Salads, endives, lettuce and chicory showed their radiant hearts, still covered by the rich garden soil; the packets of spinach and sorrel, the bunches of artichokes, the piles of beans and peas, the mounds of Romaine lettuce tied together with straw sang the entire scale of green..."

# CIMETIÈRE DU MONTPARNASSE

When the first burial took place in the cemetery of Montparnasse in 1824, it still lay outside the city boundaries. Today, it lies at the foot of the soaring new buildings of Montparnasse. Occupying an area of 20 hectares, it is not only one of the biggest cemeteries in Paris, but also a huge green area with more than 1,200 trees. Numerous famous people of varying nationalities have found their final resting place here over the years, including Irish writer Samuel Beckett, Romanian author Eugène Ionesco, American actress Jean Seberg and, of course, numerous French citizens of celebrity stature such as Charles Garnier, architect of the Opéra that bears his name, and singer Serge Gainsbourg, whose grave is one of those that attracts the most visitors. You can also see works by famous sculptors in the cemetery including Rodin, Jean Arp and Niki de Saint-Phalle.

"Wander weary, where will I / Find that final rest of mine? / Where the southern palms soar high? / Under lindens on the Rhine? // Will I die in some wild land / Buried by a stranger, or / Will I rest beneath the sand / Of some distant ocean shore? / Well, no matter! God's same sky / Will be round me, there as here / And at night the stars on high / Will be lamps to light my bier."
(Heinrich Heine in his poem "Where?")

# THE "OTHER" COUPLE: JEAN-PAUL SARTRE AND SIMONE DE BEAUVOIR

Dig deep into the golden years of Saint-Germain-des-Prés and you will find that all roads lead to Simone de Beauvoir (1908–1986) and Jean-Paul Sartre (1905–1980). Sartre, above all, was the literary hub around which the philosophical world of existentialism rotated. Sartre and de Beauvoir met in 1929, and had a long, but open, relationship until Sartre's death. Both kept their own apartments their whole lives. They frequently met in the cafés of Saint-Germain-des-Prés, including the Deux Magots or the Café de Flore, where they worked on their books. The works of Simone de Beauvoir are strongly characterized by feminist ideas, including *Memoirs of a Dutiful Daughter*, or her "roman-à-clef" set in Saint-Germain, *The Mandarins*. Both Sartre and de Beauvoir deplored conformity and bourgeois lifestyles, thereby strongly challenging their own upbringings. Sartre published philosophical works (*Being and Nothingness*) as well as novels (*Nausea*) and dramas (*The Flies*, *No Exit*) and always stood by his pro-Communist political convictions and principles. In 1964, he refused the Nobel Prize for Literature and his support for the demonstrators in the political unrest in May 1968 caused a sensation, as did his visit to Andreas Baader, a member of the extreme-left Red Army Faction, in prison in Stuttgart-Stammheim.

# THE "OTHER" COUPLE: JEAN-PAUL SARTRE AND SIMONE DE BEAUVOIR

"What is a woman?" asked Simone de Beauvoir in her groundbreaking work *The Other Sex*, in which she also determined that "One is not born as a woman, one becomes it". She also tried with Jean-Paul Sartre to define an "open" relationship, with whom she could "enjoy the advantages of a life together, but none of the discomforts" – they had separate apartments.

# A QUESTION OF ATTITUDE: LE BISTRO

Some legends may sound too good to be true, for example the one that claims the bistro, the most French of all institutions, owes its name to wealthy Russian émigrés who fled to France in 1917, before the storm of the October Revolution, with little of their money but a good deal of aristocratic arrogance. They were supposedly wont to call out to the waiters "bystro, bystro," which means "quickly, quickly" in Russian. According to another version, it happened much earlier: the Cossacks, who occupied Paris in 1814/1815, during the Napoleonic Wars, are said to have called out "bystro, bystro" in the taverns of the time. So the question as to the true identity of "the" bistro remains unanswered. Or, to put the question differently: What are they, and if so, how many are there? The answer might be: Bistros that truly deserve the title are the places where, like a Viennese coffeehouse, you feel "at home without being at home". Others often talk about the "Salon of the little people," but does that really help? A "real" bistro is more of an attitude toward life, where printed menus (instead of a board with a menu written in chalk) and smoke-free zones around the "zinc" bar-counter are likely to shatter the world view of even the most benevolently-inclined bistro habitué. Nonetheless, he will doubtlessly continue to return to "his" bistro.

"The French see food as an enrichment of the everyday routine", wrote Friedrich Sieburg – distinguishing between bistros, brasseries and restaurants. The least expensive is the bistro, followed by the brasserie; the less said about prices in some restaurants, the better. "Hareng baltique" is an essential component of the menu of a "classic" bistro – a herring swimming in cold olive oil with lukewarm boiled potatoes.

# BOULEVARD SAINT-GERMAIN

No, she didn't regret anything, sang Edith Piaf in the 1960s, echoing the mood that has always prevailed on the Boulevard Saint-Germain, namely *savoir-vivre*, in a place where once the protagonists of the Enlightenment gathered, where Delacroix arranged musical evenings in his backyard studio with Frédéric Chopin, where black-clad existentialists surrounded Jean-Paul Sartre and Simone de Beauvoir in debate, and where, to this day, travellers from all over the world explore the "golden triangle of Saint-Germain-des-Prés", between exclusive boutiques and galleries; where the mainstays are the Brasserie Lipp (now the "Brasserie des Bords du Rhin"), the Café des Deux Magots and the Café de Flore. They are all still searching for a lifestyle, perhaps for a myth from a time when the sparrow of Paris sang from the rooftops: "Non, je ne regrette rien."

The meadows that once surrounded the Abbey of Saint-Germain-des-Prés have long since been built up, and the boulevard of the same name is bustling with life by day and by night. Some of the cafés and bistros, however, continue to profit from the legends. It is said that Albert Camus always referred to a philosophically-inclined waiter in the Café de Flore on the corner of Rue Saint-Benoît as "Descartes".

# CHANSON D'AMOUR: BRINGING THE SOUL TO LIFE

The French *Chanson* has a long tradition. Historians have traced its roots back to François Villon (ca. mid-15th century), the rebellious poet of the late Middle Ages, whose "Ballade des Dames du Temps Jadis" was put to music in 1954 by Georges Brassens. At the start of the 20th century, the mecca of *chanson* was still Montmartre, with Mistinguett and Maurice Chevalier setting the pace. In the 1930s and 1940s, singers like Charles Trenet and Lucienne Boyer were joined by singer / actors such as Jean Gabin, Fernandel and Arletty, whose songs are not very well known outside France. In the postwar era, the cozy venues of Saint-Germain-des-Prés and the Quartier Latin served as a springboard for several international careers. The songs of Edith Piaf, Juliette Gréco, Georges Brassens, Yves Montand, Jacques Brel, Léo Ferré, Gilbert Bécaud, Charles Aznavour, Jean Ferrat and Georges Moustaki, for example, are still loved around the world. But the most important venue in French entertainment is not on the Left Bank; it is on the opposite bank of the Seine on the Boulevard des Capucines at the Olympia, not far from the opéra. A frail Edith Piaf appeared on stage here shortly before her death in one of her legendary concerts. Today, the Olympia plays host to artists from Leonard Cohen to Madonna.

## CHANSON D'AMOUR: BRINGING THE SOUL TO LIFE

Legendary singers of the French *chanson* who have gained international renown include Juliette Gréco (left), Charles Aznavour (below left) and Léo Ferré (below). "Unfortunately, we speak the truth," it was said in François Truffaut's film *The Woman Next Door*, but this truth is perhaps less in the lyrics and notes than in the people who sing them and bring our souls to life.

# THE INSTITUT DE FRANCE AND THE "IMMORTALS"

The country's intellectual élite gathers at the Institut de France. Its lofty conception of itself as the "Parliament of the scientific world" is more of a definition of its aims: "to perfect the arts and sciences in accordance with the principles of the diversity of disciplines." The institute was founded in 1795 to revive the royal academies, which had been dissolved during the Revolution, under a common umbrella organization: the Académie française (founded in 1635), Académie des inscriptions et belles-lettres (1663), Académie des sciences (1666), Académie des Beaux-Arts (founded in 1816 by the fusion of two older academies) and the Académie des sciences morales et politiques (1795). Since 1805, the think tank has been housed in the Collège des Quatre Nations, designed by Louis Le Vau (1612–1670) and completed in 1682; it lies opposite the Louvre and functions as the Baroque counterpart to the latter. Most famous is the Académie française: its forty members, whose main task is to publish a dictionary of the French language, are known as the "Immortals", because they are appointed for life. Each newly elected member gives a eulogy praising the deceased member, which is answered by one of the "Immortals". The first woman in the illustrious circle was Marguerite Yourcenar in 1980 (1903–1987).

# THE INSTITUT DE FRANCE AND THE "IMMORTALS"

The majesty of the building (seen here with the Pont des Arts in the foreground) is as magnificent as the claim: "... only France possesses an institute that unites all the aspirations of the human intellect, in which poets, philosophers, historians, critics, mathematicians, physicists, astronomers, scientists, economists, lawyers, painters and musicians meet together in a collegial manner."

# MUSÉE D'ORSAY

When the Gare d'Orsay was opened in 1900 for the World Expo, it was regarded as one of the most modern railway stations in France, but by the end of the 1930s, the building could no longer handle the technological developments of the railways and was closed down. In 1978, the state declared the building a historic monument, and from 1980 it was transformed into a museum, the design for which was done by Milan-based architect Gae Aulenti in 1982. She used the glass roof of the former station concourse to create a bright central space with primarily natural lighting. Today, the museum exhibits masterpieces of French art, most of which date from the second half of the 19th century. Most importantly, however, is the world-famous collection of Impressionist works, with treasures including masterpieces by Degas, Manet, Monet, Pissarro and Renoir.

Both inside and out (left), the museum that has been housed here since 1986 makes no attempt to conceal its origins – the redesign largely preserved the structures of the former railway station. Its art collection covers the years 1848–1914, and provides a link between the collections in the Louvre and those in the Musée National d'Art Contemporain (Centre Pompidou).

# HERALDS OF THE MODERN AGE: PAUL GAUGUIN, VINCENT VAN GOGH

After the establishment of the Second Republic in 1848, and before the outbreak of World War I in 1914, Paris was a center for the avant-garde movement. The Realist, Naturalist and Impressionist works of its artists triumphed over the Classicism of the previous era and developed into a contemporary art that was more in tune with the times. Among the artists of the movement was Paris-born Paul Gauguin (1848–1903), who ulti-mately created his most prominent works outside the metropolis on the Seine, in Provençe. Indeed, it was in Arles that he discovered his own style, inspired to a great degree by the light of the natural landscape. Gauguin worked in Brittany after that, especially in Pont-Aven, and from 1891 he set himself up in Polynesia. Dutch painter Vincent van Gogh (1853–1890) was lured to Paris in 1886 by his brother Theo, who was an art dealer there. He painted primarily city scenes, landscapes and portraits while there, pictures that solidified his role as one of the founders of modern painting, together with Gauguin (and Cézanne). In 1888, he too went to Arles, but his cooperation with Paul Gauguin, whom he greatly admired, in the "Atelier of the South," ended in disaster. Van Gogh suffered a nervous breakdown and committed suicide in 1890, just two years later, in Auvers near Paris.

# HERALDS OF THE MODERN AGE: PAUL GAUGUIN, VINCENT VAN GOGH

Among the highlights of the collection in the Musée d'Orsay is van Gogh's *Self-Portrait* from 1889, one year before his death (below). Also on view are his *Portrait of Dr. Paul Gachet* and *The Church at Auvers* (below left and center), both produced the year the artist died. The museum also shows Paul Gauguin's paintings *The Meal*, created in 1891, and *Women on the Beach* (in Tahiti, left).

# AHEAD OF ITS TIME: "THE IMPRESSIONIST EYE"

In Paris you will not only find one of the most important collections of Impressionist paintings in the world (in the Musée d'Orsay), but also the painting that gave the movement its name (in the Musée Marmottan), albeit unintentionally at first: Claude Monet's Impression, soleil levant (Impression, Sunrise). When Monet first showed the painting in 1872, in an exhibition arranged by artists who had been rejected by established organizers, it provoked a critic to remark, "These Impressionists are incapable of producing anything." This may not have been a very well-founded observation, but it was shared by a large majority of the public at the time. In fact, the Impressionists not only abandoned the academic studio painting of the 19th century, they also physically left their own studios in order to paint nature scenes outside. They also differ from the "academics" with regards to their brushwork and choice of perspective. Very few contemporaries at the time recognized that they were entering new artistic territory, but one of them, author Jules Laforgue (1860–1884), commented that, "The Impressionist eye is the one that is furthest ahead in human development; it is the eye that has perceived the most complicated connections of nuances and colors and managed to reproduce them on canvas."

# AHEAD OF ITS TIME: "THE IMPRESSIONIST EYE"

When the first Impressionist exhibition opened in Paris in April 1874, virtually no one guessed that it would lead to a new, and very successful, movement. Today, the struggle for recognition by artists like Claude Monet (left: The Field of Poppies, 1873), Edgar Degas (below left: The Dance Foyer at the Opera on the rue Le Peletier) and Auguste Renoir (below: Dance in the City, 1883) is long since forgotten.

# PALAIS BOURBON

The original palace, the core of which has been mostly retained, was built between 1722 and 1728 for Louise Françoise de Bourbon, daughter of King Louis XIV. In 1765, her grandson and heir, the Prince de Condé, extended the complex based on a design by Jacques-Germain Soufflot. Under state control during the French Revolution, a classical portico was later added that mirrored the Madeleine Church on the opposite bank of the Seine.

The palais has been a political meeting place since 1827, first for the Lower House of Parliament and then, from 1849, for the French National Assembly. Additional renovations were carried out to meet the requirements of the representatives; painter Eugène Delacroix – later also an elected representative – worked on the interior design. Among the historic documents held in the library are records from the trial of Joan of Arc.

In the evening, the Palais Bourbon shines thanks to the festive illumination of the building and the Seine (above). The front façade of the palace dates from the time of Napoleon I. With its columns and triangular gables, it was modelled on antique temples (large picture). Statues of the goddesses of wisdom and justice flank the outside staircase. If you want to see the interior, you have to register in advance.

# MUSÉE RODIN

The Musée Rodin is located in the Hôtel Biron, a large palace built in the rococo style by Jean Aubert in 1729–30. A famous sculptor and painter, Auguste Rodin rented rooms here in 1908 on the recommendation of his secretary, German poet Rainer Maria Rilke; the spacious building already contained an artist's studio. In 1911, the state took over the building and the residents were forced out, but Rodin was reluctant to leave the neighbor-hood and was eventually granted the right to live in the building for the rest of his life – in return for the donation of his estate. Considered a pioneer of modern art, Rodin died in 1917, and the museum opened in 1919. In addition to his works, you can see paintings and drawings that he collected over the years, as well as works by his student and former lover, Camille Claudel, the sister of poet Paul Claudel.

Rodin's study for *The Burghers of Calais* (left), clearly demonstrated his artistic credo that primary forms exist, and they would cease to do so, if he were to work with the intention of completing them based on outward appearance. The Musée Rodin (below, the garden) features one of the artist's most famous works, *The Kiss* (far left), a marble sculpture of unsurpassable intimate expression.

# HÔTEL AND DÔME DES INVALIDES

Louis XIV built the Hôtel des Invalides as a hospital for wounded soldiers. A highlight of the building complex, designed by Libéral Bruant and completed in 1676, is the church constructed in the last decades of the 17th century based on designs by Jules Hardouin-Mansart. Its impressive cupola was regilded in 1989 for the bicentennial of the Revolution. Directly below the cupola is the red marble sarcophagus of Emperor Napoleon I, which conceals five further coffins made from tinplate, mahogany, lead, ebony and oak. His remains were brought to Paris from St Helena in 1840 and interred beneath the dome in 1861. The Hôtel des Invalides is also home to several other specialty museums: the Musée de l'Armée, the Musée de l'Ordre de la Libération, the Musée d'Histoire Contemporaine, and the Musée des Plans et des Reliefs.

# HÔTEL AND DÔME DES INVALIDES

The dome of Les Invalides (far left) pierces the sky on the Left Bank of the Seine. At 101 m (335 ft), the central cupola is an integral element in the cityscape. Its pastel-colored fresco was painted by baroque artist Charles de la Fosse (left). The Cathedral of Saint-Louis des Invalides (below), which includes the Soldiers' Church and the Dome's Church, forms a part of the Invalides complex.

# "EMPEROR OF THE FRENCH": NAPOLEON BONAPARTE

It is said that Napoleon once observed, "history is the lie which we have all agreed upon." His rise to power was meteoric: Born on August 15, 1769, in Ajaccio, Corsica, Napoleone Buonaparte was already at the military academy in Paris by 1785, and within ten years he was already a Brigadier General. Another decade on, he crowned himself "Emperor of the French", and by the time ten more years had passed he had almost all of Europe and parts of North Africa under his tutelage. Napoleon's fall came quickly, however, despite a string of military successes in Austria, Prussia and Russia. Having got his army stuck too deeply in the Russian winter, it was decimated by disease and defeated in the Battle of Leipzig in 1813 during a retreat. Under pressure from the victorious powers, Napoleon was forced to abdicate the throne and was exiled to the island of Elba in 1814. He returned a year later, but 100 days after that his army was defeated again at Waterloo in Belgium. That sealed his fate: In 1815 the English banned him to the British island of St Helena, far out in the South Atlantic. He died there of stomach cancer on May 5, 1821. His body was exhumed in 1840 and reburied in the Dôme des Invalides in a magnificent sarcophagus.

# "EMPEROR OF THE FRENCH": NAPOLEON BONAPARTE

Napoleon's mortal remains lie in the Dôme des Invalides in five sarcophaguses, the outer one of which is made of brownish-red quartzite (left). Jacques-Louis David, an artist with close links to the Revolution, portrayed the coronation ceremony of Napoleon and Joséphine in 1804 (below left), while Paul Delaroche painted a portrait of the Corsica native in his study (below).

# THE EIFFEL TOWER

179 RIVE GAUCHE

# THE EIFFEL TOWER

# THE EIFFEL TOWER

In the French consciousness, the French Revolution was a unique event. They therefore planned the 1889 World Exposition in Paris to gloriously mark its 100th anniversary. Work on the world's tallest structure, the Eiffel Tower, began in 1887. Named for the engineer who built it, Gustave Eiffel, the spire was erected in record time by some 3,000 metalworkers who assembled the steel framework construction using almost 20,000 industrially pre-fabricated components and some 2.5 million rivets. Sceptics were proved wrong, and the tower survived every storm. Paris now had a new landmark that the world could see as an example of the achievements of modern architecture. Since then, every seven years the tower's outward appearance is revived with some sixty tons of paint. It is particularly attractive at night, when it is illuminated with a flashing beacon at the top.

# THE EIFFEL TOWER

Alexandre Gustave Eiffel got his idea for the Eiffel Tower from his colleagues Maurice Koechlin and Emile Nougier. By dividing it into three sections and adding rounded arches, architect Stephen Sauvestre gave the construction transparency. His design so delighted Eiffel that he took over the entire project. The tower was to be demolished after the Expo, but because it could be used as a radio tower, it was spared.

# AT THE TOP IN HIS TIME: GUSTAVE EIFFEL

Born in Dijon in 1832, Gustave Eiffel studied at the École centrale des arts et manufactures in Paris, where he received a diploma in chemical engineering in 1855. This was followed by an apprenticeship at an ironworks, which aroused his interest in metals. In 1856, steel construction developer Charles Nepveu employed the young engineer in his railway bridge construction department. The first important project supervised by Eiffel was the railway bridge in Bordeaux. In 1866, Eiffel became an independent contractor, executing further projects not only in France but throughout Europe (Hungary, Romania, Portugal, Switzerland) and South America. Apart from the Eiffel Tower, he was involved in the development of the steel skeleton for the Statue of Liberty, now in New York and completed in 1886 – this famous symbol of freedom in the United States was, in fact, a gift from the people of France. Still, Eiffel's name will always be linked first and foremost with his iconic tower in Paris, where he demonstrated a basic premise of modern architecture: that technology and functionality belong together, and when combined they can even develop a certain aesthetic presence. The engineer incidentally had a very strong attachment to "his" tower and even built a small flat for himself inside it.

# AT THE TOP IN HIS TIME: GUSTAVE EIFFEL

Eiffel (1832–1923), a descendant of German immigrants, was an energetic businessman. In addition to the world-famous tower in Paris that bears his name, he and his Paris office built further projects in France and abroad, even in Africa and South America. Typical Eiffel projects followed the "qraphic style", which was new in those days, and were thus also aesthetically on the cutting edge of their time.

# ÉCOLE MILITAIRE

If you stand on the banks of the Seine and look through the base pillars of the Eiffel Tower, directly behind the Champ de Mars you will see a powerful building, surmounted by a central dome, and with an unadorned façade and portico supported by Corinthian columns. Jacques-Ange Gabriel was responsible for the design of the military academy, built between 1759 and 1782 as the headquarters of the academy founded by King Louis XV in 1751 to educate young officers. It was from this academy that Lieutenant Napoleon Bonaparte began his meteoric rise in the military in 1785. Within the building complex of the École Militaire stands the Chapelle St Louis, also built based on Gabriel's designs. It is decorated with reliefs by Augustin Pajou and paintings by Joseph-Marie Vien, Charles André van Loo and other famous artists.

The building complex of the École Militaire, including the main courtyard, is much larger than it looks through the Eiffel Tower. Its numerous military education and training institutions are not open to the public, but there are a few reminders of the past inside (left); visitors interested in military history should definitely make a point of visiting the Musee de l'Armée, which is near the Dôme des Invalides.

# MUSÉE DU QUAI BRANLY

The Musée du Quai Branly is also called the "Musée des Arts et Civilisations d'Afrique, d'Asie, d'Océanie et des Amériques". The establishment was initially greeted with universal skepticism. The first plans for the building were produced in 1990, when Jacques Chirac was still the Mayor of Paris. Five years later, when Chirac became France's president, he pursued the project, which was intended to unite the ethnological collections of the Musée de l'Homme and the Musée National des Arts d'Afrique et d'Océanie under a single roof. Jean Nouvel designed the building for the ultramodern Ethnological Museum, whose roughly 300,000 exhibits have been a magnet for the public since its opening on June 20, 2006. It provides insight into the ethnic groups and areas of settlement on five continents: Africa, Asia, Oceania and North and South America.

The ethnological collection here is presented with the latest educational ideals in mind, introducing ancient civilizations, art, religion, cults and customs that lie beyond the familiar canon of Western cultural identity. The information is thus presented in an entertaining and informative way. Beneath the main gallery mounted on pillars, there is a garden where you can relax and reflect on what you have seen.

# THE PARIS WORLD EXPOS

Back in the days when television had not yet begun bringing pictures from all over the world into our living rooms, and long-distance travel was still beyond the reach of most pocketbooks, the World Expo served as an important source of otherwise unavailable information. Many of them also brought new buildings or other innovations to the host town, which were then kept on a permanent basis. Paris was no different. In fact, a whole series of World Expos took place here, in 1855, 1867, 1878, 1889, 1900, 1925 and 1937. The first Bateaux-Mouches (lit.: "fly boats"), for example, appeared on the Seine as a result of the 1867 World Expo – they still provide tourists and locals alike with a tranquil way to explore the river. The Palais du Trocadéro was also built for the World Expo, in 1878; however, some sixty years later, in 1937, it had to make room for the new Palais de Chaillot, which was built to mark another Expo. It was for the 1889 World Expo that Gustave Eiffel designed the tower that bears his name, which quickly became the city's most famous landmark. The first métro lines were also constructed for the World Expo, in 1900. But beyond all of these innovations, the Paris World Expos had another effect that was most welcome: they were an excellent advertising platform for the metropolis on the Seine.

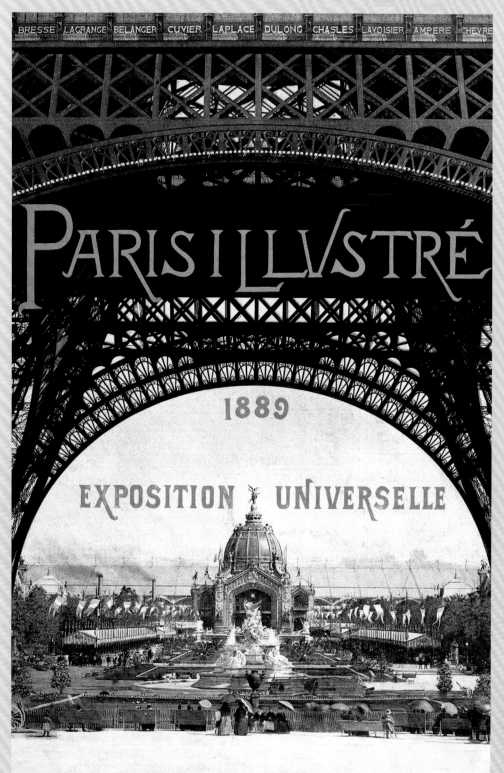

# THE PARIS WORLD EXPOS

One of the main attractions at the 1889 Universal Exhibition was the Palais des Beaux-Arts and the Arts Libéraux on the Champ de Mars (far left). Left: A woodcut shows the Sculpture Hall in the Grand Palais at the Paris 1900 World's Fair. Other artistic testimonies of the 1889 Exposition Universelle are the advertising poster and an illustration depicting the colourful spectacle of the fountain complex (bottom left).

# ÎLE AUX CYGNES

The Île des Cygnes can be rather confusing. In fact, the original island bearing this name no longer exists – it was connected to the nearby river bank, the Champ de Mars, even before the Revolution. Today's Île des Cygnes is a reclaimed area 890 m (264 ft) long and almost 20 m (66 ) wide that offers a pleasant place to stroll beneath the trees with a view of the Maison de Radio France. At the southern end of the island is a replica of the Statue of Liberty in New York, a reminder of the original, which was donated to the United States by France. The replica is only a quarter of the size of its "big sister". At the request of the sculptor Auguste Bartholdi, it was positioned so that it looks westwards. On the book in her hand is the inscription "IV Juillet 1776 = XIV Juillet 1789". These are the dates of the American and French revolutions, respectively.

On the Île des Cygnes, surprised visitors may wonder if they have been transported to New York – a replica of the Statue of Liberty stands here. But the Paris copy is only 11.5 m (38 ft) high and the original measures 46.5 m (154 ft). At the northern end of the Île des Cygnes is the equestrian statue *La France renaissante* (1930, below) which will remove any remaining doubts of one's location.

# BEYOND THE CENTER

The city center, stretched along the left and right banks of the Seine, is a real treasure trove of architectural masterpieces, museums and romantic squares. Beyond that, Paris spreads out in all directions as far as the ring motorway (La Périphérique), which has long since served the boundary function once fulfilled by the old city walls. On both sides, you will find yourself plunged into a wide variety of environments, from the gracious alleys of Montmartre around Sacré-Cœur to the spectacular Parc de la Villette, and from the rural idyll of the Bois de Boulogne to the skyscrapers of La Défense.

The Grande Arche was completed in 1989 to mark the bicentennial of the French Revolution. It marks the end of the "Axe historique" and was one of President Mitterrand's pet building projects; it was designed by Johan Otto von Spreckelsen and Paul Andreu.

# BOIS DE BOULOGNE

From royal hunting grounds to the city's green lung: The Bois de Boulogne measures some 850 ha (2,100 acres) and was given the name "Forest of Boulogne", after the pilgrimage church Notre-Dame-de-Boulogne-le-Petit, which Philippe IV had built in 1308 after returning from a pilgrimage to Boulogne-sur-Mer. In 1556, under Henri II, the forest was surrounded by a wall with eight gates; the first roads were laid under Louis XIV and the area was opened to the public. In 1852, Napoleon III ordered the walls to be demolished and commissioned Haussmann to redesign the park. Today, this oasis of green on the western edge of the city, with its lakes and waterfalls, shady avenues, footpaths and gardens is a popular recreation area by day, while at night the Bois de Boulogne becomes a hunting ground once more – for the oldest profession in the world.

The Bois de Boulogne (below) was modelled on Hyde Park in London. The Parc de Bagatelle (above) is especially worth a visit. It was created in 1775 as the result of a wager between the Count d'Artois, who later became Charles X, and his sister-in-law, Marie-Antoinette, in which the challenge was to build a castle with gardens in record time; in less than three months the plan had been carried out.

# PARIS TRAIN STATIONS

All the main stations in Paris are termini, which means trains typically end here. Locals maintain that this is intentional, because people arriving in Paris never want to continue on anywhere else anyway. However, if you do want to travel to other parts of the country, you have to take the métro to a different station. Trains from Northern France and Belgium, for example, arrive at Gare du Nord; from Alsace and Germany at Gare de l'Est; from southern France and Italy you come into Gare de Lyon; from central France it is Gare d'Austerlitz; from western and south-western France you arrive at Gare Montparnasse; and from Normandy at Gare Saint-Lazare. All the major stations were built between the mid-19th and early 20th century, magnificent structures that have largely retained their original designs; only Gare Montparnasse has had a modern building with a glass façade added to it. Gare de Lyon also attracts gourmets with its restaurant "Le Train Bleu", where they can dine in a magnificently decorated room with a (painted) backdrop of places in southern France. Gare d'Orsay, like Gare de Lyon, was built for the 1900 World Expo. It was later rebuilt in the 1980s and is now one of the city's most frequently-visited museums with a display of Impressionist works.

"So must our fathers have felt when America was discovered ..." wrote Heinrich Heine, when the first train travelled from Paris to Orléans in 1843. "The railroads again are such an event that they give humanity a new impetus ..." Three years later, Gare du Nord (left, below left) was opened and Gare de Lyon followed six years later (below: "Le Train Bleu" restaurant and Gare de l'Est).

# LA DÉFENSE

Plans for the great commercial district to the west of Paris began in the mid-1950s, and the first building, the CNIT (Centre de Nouvelles Industries et Technologies), opened in 1958. The first high-rises appeared in the 1970s, provoking a storm of protest as they spoiled the view from the Champs-Élysées to the west. In the 1980s, the tower blocks multiplied and grew skyward, and today many major French companies have their headquarters here.

The architectural jewel in the crown, the Grande Arche, was opened in 1989 for the bicentennial celebration of the French Revolution. This completed the "Axe Historique", an historical line of sight running through the western part of the city, from the Arc de Triomphe du Carrousel near the Louvre, through the Arc de Triomphe and on to the Grande Arche on Place Charles de Gaulle at the top of the Champs-Élysées.

Glass and steel are the dominant materials in the Quartier La Défense (left), where skyscrapers such as the Tour T1 and the B Building (both 2008), the Tour Generali and the Tour Granite (both 2011), and the Tour Phare define the modern skyline. Sculptures in the area are a relaxing contrast to the stark architecture and give it an open-air museum feel. Below: the *Tête monumentale* by Polish sculptor Igor Mitoraj.

# LEGENDARY MONTMARTRE

More than any other district of Paris, Montmartre – the "Butte", as locals call this barely 130-m-high (430-ft) "hill" – has two personalities. On the one side is the almost village-like idyll that it seems to maintain, including its own vineyard, while on the other is the Montmartre you will find around the Place du Tertre, which has long since been a caricature of itself. Many Paris fans will recall the story of the first bishop of the city, Saint Dionysius (and his two companions), who were martyred on Montmartre in about 250, before miraculously walking some six kilometers toward what is now Saint-Denis with his decapitated head under his arm. According to this legend, the name of the district is derived from the Latin "Mons Martyrorum" (Mountain of the Martyrs), which refers to this event. However, the name more likely goes back to the "Mons Martis" (Mountain of Mars), from Roman times when there were two temples here dedicated to the gods Mars and Mercury. These days, you will seldom encounter gods here, but miraculous things still seem to happen – such as the football freestyler, Iya Traore, from Guinea, who played his way into the hearts of fans with his amazing ball skills, which he demonstrated on the terrace in front of Sacré-Coeur.

In the little cobblestone alleys of Montmartre, you will feel you have been transported back to the days when artists like Pablo Picasso found cheap lodging and all manner of inspiration here. Cafés and restaurants like La Crémaillère 1900 jostle for your attention around the old village square, Place du Tertre, hemmed in by low houses from the 18th century.

# SACRÉ-CŒUR

After defeat in the Franco-Prussian War (1870/71), and the bloody suppression of the Paris Commune in 1871, Montmartre's history of association with martyrdom seemed to make it the ideal place for atonement among French Catholics; a place to regain political and religious purity. As such, the National Assembly declared in 1873 that a church of atonement should be erected here and dedicated to the Sacred Heart of Jesus: Sacré-Cœur.

Funds for its construction were collected in a national fundraising campaign that began in 1876, but was not completed until 1914 – long after the death of the appointed architect, Paul Abadie (1812–1884). Drawing on unlimited stylistic resources, Abadie had created in Sacré-Cœur a total work of art bringing together Byzantine, Moorish, Gothic and Romanesque elements. Indeed, it is impossible to imagine the city without it.

Sacré-Cœur rises majestically atop Montmartre, and its terraced steps afford one of the loveliest views of the City of Light. The mosaic of Christ in the choir vault was created by Luc-Olivier Merson as an expression of the veneration of the Sacred Heart. Sacré-Cœur owes it radiant color to the mineral calcite, which is exuded by the travertine building materials when exposed to the elements, lending it a chalky whiteness.

# HENRI DE TOULOUSE-LAUTREC: CHRONICLER OF PARIS SOCIETY

Henri de Toulouse-Lautrec was born in 1864 in Albi, southern France, the son of one of France's oldest aristocratic families. "I have tried to be truthful, and to not distort anything, as if in a dream," he observed as a young man, when formulating his artistic approach. "Perhaps that is a mistake, but I find it impossible to ignore warts; I even mischievously add a few hairs; I like to make them larger and give them a shiny top." Since his growth was stunted by two broken legs sustained in a number of riding accidents in his youth, he began drawing at an early age and began a course of study in Paris in 1882. He soon found the ideal backdrop for his paintings in Montmartre and became one of the most critical chroniclers of Paris society at the end of the 19th century. Taking influences from Edgar Degas as well as from colored Japanese woodcuts, Toulouse-Lautrec developed his own style, the most important characteristics of which were a diagonal line of composition, the absence of shadow, people cut off at the edges of the picture, and reduced contours – these were also characteristic of the color lithographs and posters he produced in the 1890s. Henri de Toulouse-Lautrec had a decisive influence on the overall development of Art Nouveau. He died in 1901 shortly before his 37th birthday.

# HENRI DE TOULOUSE-LAUTREC: CHRONICLER OF PARIS SOCIETY

Henri de Toulouse-Lautrec is famous above all for his posters from the Montmartre cabaret scene. In many of them, performers like dancer Jane Avril (below left), chansonnier Aristide Bruant (below) and the can-can dancer La Goulue (far left) are the main focus. The seated figure (left) shows Cha-u-ka-o, the female clown of the "Moulin Rouge".

# OF HABITUÉS, TRENDY DISTRICTS AND LONGINGS

New York uses it as an advertisement, but in Paris no one even mentions it: "sex and the city". That is to say, people don't "talk" about it in Paris. The city is simply sexy, especially where it is not on display in glaringly large letters, like at the shops and shows of the honey-pot around Place Pigalle, which still lures countless voyeurs; or in the up-market hangouts like the Moulin Rouge in Montmartre, which has been open since 1889; or at the Lido on the Champs-Élysées (since 1946); or the Crazy Horse in elegant Avenue George V (since 1951); or the Folies Bergère in Rue Richter, founded in 1870 as the first establishment of its kind, where modestly staged nudity seems the very opposite of erotic. Instead of heading off into a world that often only retains the cliché images of the pleasure establishments, dance cafés, cabarets and bordellos in which Toulouse-Lautrec once found his models and model types, you may be better served following the tracks of the local habitués, a tour of which would likely begin at the Bastille and end in the "wild east", in Belleville, in the wee hours, taking you from Rue de Charonne, along the quays of Canal St-Martin to Rue Oberkampf – there is something for everyone here, even if they are in search of desire itself.

"Only in the evening do the spots and neon lights arouse in the visitor an illusion of being in a playful X-rated film, when he thinks he can spy out the much envied purgatory of the voluptuaries and not fall into the fire himself ..." wrote Wolfgang Koeppen, coming then to his own personal conclusion that "only he who is content to observe the fair will find what he is looking for."

# SAINT-OUEN

The northern suburb of Saint-Ouen has few remarkable sights to offer, but many Parisians still take the long métro ride out there. The reason is the Marché aux Puces de Saint-Ouen, one of the world's largest flea markets. It is held every Saturday, Sunday and Monday between the Porte de Clignancourt and the Porte de Saint-Ouen, and offers antiques and bric à brac to suit virtually any taste or style. Cemetery visitors travel occasionally to these suburbs. The little cemetery of Saint-Ouen, for example, is home not only to the graves of artists like Suzanne Valadon (1865–1938, a painter and Toulouse-Lautrec muse who worked in nearby Montmartre), but also of writer Ödön von Horváth, who was killed by a falling branch during a thunderstorm on the Champs-Élysées in 1938.

Spread out over a massive area, the Marché aux Puces de Saint-Ouen has something for everyone, and of course collectors, treasure hunters and bargain-seekers have to work their way through an enormous amount of junk before they find something of value. But there are some rare and hard-to-find items out there if you have the time to look for them.

# CANAL SAINT-MARTIN

A stroll along the Canal Saint-Martin introduces visitors to a different Paris, far removed from the historic buildings and iconic monuments of the city center. On the streets around the canal you can still find artisans and traders enjoying a coffee or an aperitif at a local bar, or generally going about their business. Fans of French cinema may recognize the Canal Saint-Martin – or its studio replica – as the backdrop for the 1938 classic *Hôtel du Nord* by French director Marcel Carnés. Built between 1805 and 1825, on orders from Napoleon, it is still possible to take a boat trip on the canal, part of which leads underground – the canal is covered from Rue du Faubourg du Temple to the Place de la Bastille. Lasting around two hours, the trips run from the Bassin de la Villette in the north to the Bassin de l'Arsenal, the dock of the Bastille, where the canal enters the Seine.

Nine weirs navigate an elevation difference of 25 m (82 ft) on the 4.5-km (2.8-mi) Canal Saint-Martin, which can be crossed on a footbridge at the Quai de Valmy (below). Graffiti writers flock to the riverbank to express themselves (left). The canal is not just a place of enjoyment and recreation, however. The Paris fire department divers practice here as well.

# CIMETIÈRE DU PÈRE-LACHAISE

The cemeteries in Paris used to be on lots adjacent to churches, but with time they grew overcrowded and eventually became a dangerous health hazard. As a result, Napoleon ordered the construction of three cemeteries on the edge of the city in 1804: Montparnasse, Montmartre and Père-Lachaise. The latter was built on land owned by the father confessor of Louis XIV, Père de La Chaize. Père-Lachaise is now the largest cemetery in Paris, covering 43 ha (106 acres). Numerous celebrities are buried here – or were reburied – including the dramatist Molière, the poet Jean de La Fontaine, and Abélard and Héloïse, the ill-fated 12th-century lovers. More recent interments include the Doors singer Jim Morrison, Edith Piaf, Oscar Wilde, and Simone Signoret and Yves Montand. Maps of the graves are available at kiosks and shops close to the entrance.

The Père-Lachaise Cemetery is also called the "Haute École des Morts", or the "Academy of the Dead": This refers to the many celebrities buried or reburied here, including Jim Morrison (on the left a picture taken after the theft of his bust), Frédéric Chopin (top right) and the French artist Vivant Denon (bottom right). In the center is one of the imposing grave sculptures.

# EDITH PIAF: THE "LITTLE SPARROW"

"The people we love are not dead," commented Charles Dumont, who composed the world-famous song "Non, je ne regrette rien" for Edith Piaf. His words come to mind when one stands before her grave in the cemetery of Père-Lachaise. On a heavy black slab lies a large statue of Jesus, and on the right-hand side of the slab is an inscription in gold: Madame LAMBOUKAS / dite Edith Piaf / 1915–1963. Three lines and two sober dates that reveal very little about a life that is indeed hard to summarize with words and figures. On December 19, 2010, Edith Piaf would have been 95; five years later she would be celebrating her 100th birthday, and perhaps we may be permitted to dream and to imagine what would happen if she were to climb down from her cloud to attend that remarkable event. What would she tell us about her life: that she was abandoned by her mother soon after her birth, and that it was a snake charmer from a travelling circus who led her "from the street into a cabaret" and onto the world's stages. Would she smile at the thought, or even believe it that today she has become a role model for so many female performers, from Madonna to Lady Gaga? "Môme Piaf", the "Little Sparrow"?

# EDITH PIAF: THE "LITTLE SPARROW"

"The brat has everything in her throat but nothing in her feet", was supposedly what Edith Piaf's father said about her – he had wanted to make an acrobat out of her. Fortunately, he failed, and the great little singer that she became remains in our memories with songs like La vie en rose, *L'hymne à l'amour*, *Milord* and *Non, je ne regrette rien*.

# PARC DE LA VILLETTE

The Parc de la Villette was created in the 1980s, on a slightly unsavory site that had originally been used for slaughterhouses. A competition to design a new leisure park here was won by architects Bernard Tschumi and Adrian Fainsilber, and in 1986 the Cité des Sciences et de l'Industrie opened its gates. The complex contains a planetarium, library, and an interactive museum of science and technology, with something for both young and old alike. The Géode Omnimax theater and the Argonaute, a French military submarine are nearby as well. If your tastes are more cultural than technological, head for the Cité de la Musique, designed by Christian de Portzamparc; it presents the history of music from the Renaissance to the present day. The cast-iron Grande Halle, the original slaughterhouse dating from 1867, is now a multi-purpose venue.

The most striking building in the modern Parc de la Villette is the futuristic sphere of the Géode, a building clad in stainless steel where visitors can watch documentary films on a 1,000-sq-m (10,700-sq-ft), 172-degree screen with 12-channel surround sound

# BIBLIOTHÈQUE NATIONALE DE FRANCE: SITE FRANÇOIS MITTERRAND

The new "Bibliothèque Nationale de France: site François Mitterrand" was opened in the south-eastern part of the city in December 1996, barely a year after the death of its initiator and biggest supporter. Some ten million books from the stock of the "old" National Library in Rue de Richelieu have been moved to the new buildings. Four towers, each 78 m (243 ft) high, feature glass façades that are intended to symbolize open books. Architect Dominique Perrault won the design competition for the building in 1988, and his glass "book towers" border an inner courtyard, around which the reading rooms are arranged over two floors like cloisters. There is space for 3,600 visitors: 2,000 reading places on the ground floor are reserved for researchers, while the 1,600 additional places on the first floor are available for use by the general public.

Since July 2006, Dietmar Feichtinger's bridge (below, named after Simone de Beauvoir) has linked the park at Bercy on the right bank of the Seine with the library on the left bank. Built without supporting pillars, it consists of two interlinked arches. Inside the "book towers", with their multiple layers of glass, volumes are kept in sealed containers with constant temperatures and humidity levels (left).

# MITTERRAND, THE MASTER BUILDER

During his period in office as head of state, François Mitterrand initiated a series of projects that still decisively shape the appearance of the French capital today. As early as 1981, he started the project of the "Grand Louvre", to which the museum owes its initially controversial, but now very popular glass pyramid, designed by the Chinese-American architect leoh Ming Pei. Grand Louvre, however, meant much more – the Ministry of Finance moved into its own building in Bercy, creating additional exhibition space. Art-historically important rooms, such as the Galerie d'Apollon, were also renovated. A district previously mostly avoided by tourists also received a new attraction through Mitterrand's initiative: The Grande Arche in La Défense by the architect Otto von Spreckelsen was inaugurated on July 14, 1989, for the 200th anniversary of the Revolution. La Grande Arche de la Fraternité, as is its full name, today serves as the official residence for various ministries and is mainly used as office space. At the same time, the Opéra Bastille by the Canadian architect Carlos Ott was opened. The last major project, whose completion Mitterrand did not himself experience, were the towers of the Bibliothèque Nationale François Mitterrand.

# MITTERRAND, THE MASTER BUILDER

François Mitterrand (bottom left), who ruled France as President from 1981 to 1995, has left his mark on the Parisian cityscape like hardly any of his predecessors. The glass pyramid is the most striking aspect of his "Grand Louvre" project (large picture). The Opéra Bastille (top right) was inaugurated in 1989, on the 200th anniversary of the Revolution. Top left: the Grande Arche.

# ÎLE-DE-FRANCE

Paris is an island. Historically, because the city center is on an island in the Seine, the Île de la Cité, where fishermen from the Celtic Parisii tribe once settled, and from where the city gradually expanded to include both banks. Geographically, because Paris itself forms an island, the Île-de-France, the proverbial heartland of the country that has formed around the capital. Unlike the city, the outskirts are not as popular a destination. Still, there is plenty to see here, including impressive royal palaces and, no less impressive in its own way, Disneyland Paris.

Louis XIV commissioned sculptor Jean-Baptiste Tuby to create an allegory of himself, the Sun King, for the park at Versailles. The central figure of the Bassin d'Apollo (below), *Apollo with the Chariot of the Sun*, was completed in 1670.

# CATHEDRALE SAINT-DENIS

Saint-Denis is some 11 km (7 mi) north of the city limits and is easily reached by métro or suburban train (RER). It distinguishes itself from the drab suburbs of the *Banlieue* with its unconventional university (open to students who have not passed the matriculation exam) and the futuristic stadium built for the FIFA World Cup 1998. Above all, however, it has its cathedral, the first of the great Gothic churches. Built mostly during the 12th and 13th centuries, it is locat-ed on the site where the martyr St Dionysius is allegedly buried. The story tells of his decapitation in 250 atop Montmartre, after which he carried his head under his arm to this spot. The first chapel was erected here during the fifth century over the supposed grave, but it was replaced during the seventh century by a larger abbey church. This predecessor of today's basilica of Saint-Denis also served as the burial place of the French kings.

Saint-Denis is regarded as the first example of Gothic architecture; the rose window and soaring pillars are characteristic of the style. The coronation insignia and the Oriflamme (the royal national banner and war standard of the king) were also once kept here. Left. Sculptures on the base of the tomb of Louis XII and Anne de Bretagne. The façade was designed in 1140 under the auspices of Abbé Suger.

# CHANTILLY

The village of Chantilly is 40 km (25 mi) north of Paris in a forested area and has been a possession of the Montmorency and Condé families since the Middle Ages. During the 16th century they had an old castle complex redesigned as a Renaissance palace, which was subsequently transformed into a Baroque complex and then extended during the 19th century to include the New Palace. The interior of the palace was the property of its last aris-tocratic owner, the Duc d'Aumale, who donated the property, including a magnificent garden by André Le Nôtre, to the Institut de France at the end of the 19th century. The Château de Chantilly is the seat of the Musée Condé, an impressive private collection that includes Dürer's Melancolia and the Book of Hours of the Duc de Berry. Chantilly is also famous for its race course, opened in 1834, and the associated stud farm.

# CHANTILLY

The original castle here was transformed into the imposing Château de Chantilly and surrounded by a moat, which was then made into artificial lakes within a park. The château is unique for its art collection, which hangs in the galleries and features an extraordinary number of portraits. The Cabinet des Livres, the former library of the Château de Chantilly, is in virtually mint condition.

# MALMAISON

The origins of the Château Malmaison linger in the mists of time, as does the origin of its name – "bad house". Malmaison was first documented as an estate in the mid-13th century, but the current incarnation was built in the 18th century; the interior took on its present form when Joséphine de Beauharnais, wife of Emperor Napoleon, acquired the estate in 1799 and carried out extensive renovations. She also redesigned the park, with hothouses for exotic plants and a large rose garden. After her separation from Napoleon in 1809, Joséphine returned to Malmaison where she lived until her death in 1814. Some of the furniture on display today comes from other châteaux belonging to Napoleon; only the library on the ground floor has been maintained in its original state. The emperor and his wife are also remembered in the museum at the nearby Château de Bois-Préau.

Visitors can still get a feel for the type of person Napoleon was while strolling through the park and château at Malmaison. His library (below left) is a good place to start. The castle has changed little with time (left). An unknown artist portrayed Napoleon with the château Malmaison in the background (below).

# LOUIS XIV: "THE SUN KING"

King Louis XIV (1638–1715) exemplifies absolutist rule. His grandiose displays of power, the magnificence of his court and the glamour of Versailles served as models for an entire age. He was crowned king at the age of five, but was initially subject to the regency of his mother. He later left the business of ruling the country to Cardinal Mazarin, who had been the strongman in France since the premature death of Louis XIII. When

Mazarin, the true founder of French absolutism, died in 1661, the king, who was twenty-three years old at the time, took over a centrally ruled, rigidly organized state in which the aristocracy and the middle classes had largely been deprived of all political power. Louis refined the absolute system to such an extent that all power was concentrated in him: "L'État c'est moi" ("I am the state") is one of the comments he supposedly made about him-

self. Louis' ambitions regarding foreign policy aimed at the supremacy of France within Europe. He waged war for decades against the Habsburgs, against England, and against the Netherlands. And since war has always been the most expensive passion of megalomaniacal rulers (even more expensive than the magnificence of their courts), he left a mountain of debts when he died that became a long-term problem for the country.v

Louis XIV embodied self-dramatization (left, as a child in coronation regalia in a painting by Justus van Egmont, 1651/54). The allonge wig he designed (below) became an important fashion accessory during the Baroque period. The glorification of the monarch was the goal of the portraits by Pierre Mignard (below left) and Hyacinthe Rigaud (below) in display armor and in ermine (below center).

# PROTOTYPE OF AN ABSOLUTE RESIDENCE: CHÂTEAU DE VERSAILLES

King Louis XIII originally had a little hunting palace built near the village of Versailles, with its dense forests and extensive stocks of game. His son and heir, Louis XIV, liked to spend his time there as well, so in 1661 he had the park extended and commissioned architect Louis Le Vau (1612–1670) with the systematic expansion of the palace, which commenced in 1668. The previous building from Louis XIII was not demolished, but engulfed by the new one. This resulted in the main wing of the palace, which was then extended by Le Vau's successor, Jules Hardouin-Mansart (1646–1708). The interior decoration was designed by Charles Le Brun (1619–1690). Particularly worth seeing are the palace chapel and the throne room, the apartments of the queen and the bedchamber of Louis XIV, and of course the Hall of Mirrors, which is 73 m (240 ft) long and 11 m (36 ft) wide and has seventeen arcade windows overlooking the park. The château became the prototypical residence of an absolute ruler and was the role model for many European palace residences; the name "Versailles" even became a synonym for an entire age in Europe, that of the High and Late Baroque. The palace served as a residence for the kings of France from October 1682 until 1789, the year of the French Revolution.

# PROTOTYPE OF AN ABSOLUTE RESIDENCE: CHÂTEAU DE VERSAILLES

Louis XIV often carried out his affairs of state from his bed. After 1789, the castle was abandoned, but the Hall of Mirrors (left) remained a setting for important events such as the proclamation of the German Empire (1871) and the signing of the Treaty of Versailles (1919). Below left: Battles Gallery. Bottom: The stage of the opera house.

Versailles was the political center of France for more than 100 years. After the completion of the château at the beginning of the 18th century (where more than 36,000 people and 6,000 horses allegedly worked), there were between 5,000 and 10,000 people living in the 700-odd rooms of the palace, its outbuildings and the tiny village of Versailles itself. The tenants included a large part of the French aristocracy, since the concept of absolutism required the presence of the nobility at court. Just as the palace was extended and became the prototype of an absolutist residence, the over 800-hectare palace park was also extended by André Le Nôtre, who completed it as the prototype of the French-style garden: a work of art with plants, fountains, sculptures and two little maisons de plaisance – the Grand and Petit Trianon.

"The park", wrote art historian Thorsten Droste, "is the extended representational frame of the palace." And like the palace, the park (left the Bassin d'Apollo) is an expression of absolute sentiment: the world (including nature) reflects the will and the ideas of the king. Only in the section of the park north of the Petit Trianon (below the Temple of Apollo) was nature allowed a little more freedom.

# ANDRÉ LE NÔTRE AND THE »JARDIN À LA FRANÇAISE«

Born in Paris in 1613, André Le Nôtre came from a family of landscape architects. His first great commission was the park at Château Vaux-le-Vicomte, created for Nicolas Fouquet, finance minister under Louis XIV. The park aroused the envy f the Sun King, who then decided he would create even more splendid gardens at Versailles. Louis employed Le Nôtre, and the extensive park he created at Versailles became the latter's most im-

portant creation. His name quickly became synonymous with classic, formal French garden design, and his work was imitated throughout Europe. The gardens were laid out in symmetrical designs, with avenues and paths radiating from a central point. Making use of statues, parterres, pavilions, pools, fountains, neatly clipped topiary, trees and shrubs, the overall impression was harmonious. Le Nôtre also created the gardens of the châteaux

at Chantilly, Meudon, Saint-Cloud and Sceaux, and in England he was commissioned by Charles II to submit designs for Greenwich Park, though they were not fully realized; he is believed to have served in an advisory role in the design of London's St James's Park. In Italy, he designed the park of Villa Torrigiani di Camigliano near Lucca. Le Nôtre died in 1700 in Paris, the city of his birth, and was interred in the church of Saint-Roch.

# ANDRÉ LE NÔTRE AND THE »JARDIN À LA FRANÇAISE«

The artist and his creations: André Le Nôtre (far left, a portrait by Claude Lefebvre), whose first significant project was the park at Château Vaux-le-Vicomte (left). His masterpiece, however, was Versailles Palace, a project that made him the creator of the "most beautiful garden in France", as the monument in the Jardin des Tuileries states.

# BOIS DE VINCENNES, CHÂTEAU DE VINCENNES

The Bois de Vincennes was for centuries a hunting ground for the kings of France. It is almost 850 ha (2,100 acres) and lies southeast of the city limits, marked now by the ring motorway. In the mid-19th century it was redesigned as an expansive garden in the English style, and in 1969, a charming botanical garden was added, the Parc Floral de Paris, which is planted anew each season. Since 1970, the theatrical director Ariane Mnouch-

kine has run the famous Théâtre du Soleil in the Cartoucherie. Footpaths and bridle paths lead around the two lakes in the park. Near the métro station of the same name, the Château de Vincennes provides an impressive backdrop with a former hunting lodge built at the end of the 12th century. It was extended to create a defensive castle in the 14th century and was redesigned in the Baroque style during the 17th century.

Sainte-Chapelle, the court chapel of the Château de Vincennes, is clearly Gothic in origin. After an interruption during the Revolution, the keep served as a state prison until Napoleonic times. Lac de Daumesnil (left), in the south-western section of the Bois de Vincennes, recalls the name of one of Napoleon's generals, who determinedly defended the fortress against rebels.

# DISNEYLAND RESORT PARIS

Celebrations in 2007 marked the fifteenth anniversary of the amusement park based on Mickey Mouse & Co. 30 km (21 mi) east of Paris. Originally founded as the "Euro Disney Resort", the park is now known as the "Disneyland Resort Paris". On a site extending over 2,000 ha (4,942 acres) visitors will find two leisure parks adjoining each other here: the "Disneyland Park", a "fantasy kingdom" divided into five theme areas, and the "Walt Disney Studios Park", which was only opened in 2002, and which provides visitors with an entry (and insight) into the (film) world of animation and special effects. With over fifty main attractions, the resorts were developed by 1,000 "Fantasy Designers", and the gigantic entertainment machinery is kept running by a staff of more than 12,000 employees. Those who want to visit all the live shows on a single day will need about fourteen hours to do so.

An average of 13 million annual visitors seems convincing. Every year, 500 costume parades along Main Street at Disneyland Park and on the stages of the Walt Disney Studio Parks continue to delight. They include Goofy and Donald Duck, while on the next corner Captain Hook's pirate ship lies in ambush. In the evening, Disney's enchanted kingdom gleams by the light of 400,000 lamps.

# CHÂTEAU DE VAUX-LE-VICOMTE

Some legends are simply too enticing to be left out. The region of Vaux even still lures visitors here with the slogan "The palace that aroused the envy of the Sun King". It refers, of course, to the Château de Vaux-le-Vicomte, and the comment about the Sun King being envious is apparently proven. But the legend that it was the sole reason for dismissing his finance minister, Nicolas Fouquet (1615–1680), is probably only partly true.

During the years 1656–1661, Fouquet had a magnificent residence built here near Melun, 50 km (33 mi) south-east of Paris, based on plans by architect Louis Le Vau. The park was then designed by André Le Nôtre. The full story, however, was that, amongst other things, Fouquet had misappropriated state funds, which would have driven even a king unaffected by envy to dismiss his minister.

On August 17, 1661, Nicolas Fouquet hosted an opulent celebration in honor of Louis XIV here, at which his "master" was apparently impressed by everything including the "silverware" (which was not silver, but solid gold). In that same year, the King set to work with the architect (Le Vau), the interior decorator (Le Brun) and the garden architect (Le Nôtre) of Château de Vaux-le-Viomte on his own palace, Versailles.

# CHÂTEAU AND PARC DE FONTAINEBLEAU

From the Château de Vaux-le-Vicomte it is only 15 km (9 mi) farther south to the forest of Fontainebleau. It was here in the 12th century that Louis VII had a hunting lodge built. After having been abandoned for some time, King François I ordered the lodge to be redesigned in 1528; only one tower of the original building still remains. Italian artists including Rosso Fiorentino and Francesco Primaticio were commissioned to design the interior of the new château, two figures who represent the "School of Fontainebleau", an elegant version of the Italian Mannerist style. The château was then redesigned by both Henry IV and Napoleon. For the latter it became a fateful location, however: It was in the Salon Rouge that the emperor was forced to sign his deed of abdication and, in 1814, in the so-called Cour des Adieux, he took leave of his officers before being exiled to Elba.

Château Fontainebleau overwhelms its visitors with is spacious Renaissance halls. The 80-m (264-ft) Gallery of Diana, once painted by Ambroise Dubois, is home to the library of Napoleon III from 1851. André le Nôtre designed the Grand Parterre in 1645, a terrace-like garden landscape for presentation purposes (left).

# WARLORD AND PATRON OF THE ARTS: FRANÇOIS I

King François I (1515–1547) perfectly represented the ideal of a Renaissance prince: cultivated, energetic and of "vast stature", as his contemporaries admired, but also narcissistic, power-hungry and unscrupulous. He summoned important artists like Leonardo da Vinci to his court, initiated the royal painting collection, supported learning and science, by founding the Collège de France, for example, and had magnificent palaces built. In addition to Fontainebleau, mention should be made here above all of Chambord, the largest and most spectacular of the Loire châteaux. François was the son of the Count of Angoulême and owes his coronation as king in 1515 to an arranged marriage with the only daughter of his predecessor, Louis XII. He would have liked to be crowned emperor as well, but it was the Habsburg monarch Charles V who took that honor. François immediately attacked him as part of shifting military alliances. He even signed a treaty with the Ottoman sultan and the Protestant German princes, even though within his own country he suppressed the Reformation violently. In spite of all his efforts, however, he was unable to capture Milan in the long term (and ensure dominance in Upper Italy); nor was he able to prevent France's being caught up in the "Habsburg clutch".

# WARLORD AND PATRON OF THE ARTS: FRANÇOIS I

The gallery of François I at Château de Fontainebleau was designed by Mannerist court painters. Later, these groups became known as the Fontainebleau School. Among the works were frescoes of Venus (above) and the *Allegory of Water or Allegory of Love* (below). The half-length portrait of François I (below left) is by Jean Clouet from 1535 (perhaps with his son François).

# INDEX

# PICTURE CREDITS/IMPRINT

MONACO BOOKS is an imprint of Kunth Verlag GmbH & Co KG
© Kunth Verlag GmbH & Co.KG, Munich, 2019

For distribution please contact:
Monaco Books
c/o Kunth Verlag GmbH & Co KG,
St.-Cajetan-Straße 41,
81669 München, Germany
Tel: +49.89.45 80 20 23
Fax: +49.89.45 80 20-21
info@kunth-verlag.de
www.monacobooks.com
www.kunth-verlag.de

Printed in Slovakia

Text: Robert Fischer, Christiane Gsänger, Stefan Jordan